PRAISE FOR *Divination Conjure Style*

"Mama Starr does it again! But this time, she's giving you 'eyes to see and ears to hear!' With that southern, no-nonsense tone, she brings the reader into her world in a very unique way: one that is filled with Ancestors and spirits and roots integrated into family and daily life. Mama Starr is unique in that she has a living memory of the old ways of Conjure and the way things were done. In *Divination Conjure Style,* she reveals the many ways that divination was and is traditionally done in the Deep South: from reading playing cards and throwing bones to reading wax droplets and using blue water.

"Starr says in the beginning of the book that everyone, seasoned worker or not, may learn a thing or two. My mother taught me to read the cards about twelve years ago and I've been reading the bones for ten years, having learned from a friend of the family, and I still learned something new from this book for both methods! As Mama Starr says throughout the book, this isn't an end-all to the forms of divination one can use or how you utilize the tools, this is simply the way she remembers and was taught. That memory is something that's deeply lacking in other books on Deep South Hoodoo, and Starr's wisdom brings it right on home for a new generation of hoodoos and conjurers!"

—JAKE RICHARDS, author of *Backwoods Witchcraft*

"Starr Casas is who you want behind the table when you have a problem and need clear answers. And Starr Casas is also the one you want working for you when you need that problem fixed. In *Divination Conjure Style,* she shares with you her system of practical, down-to-earth reading with playing cards, rather than Tarot or oracle decks, to get you the information you need, and shows you how to work with the cards to change your situation. From prepping and setting up to reading the layout, you'll feel as if Starr is talking to you and guiding you on the path."

—CHRISTOPHER PENCZAK, cofounder of the Temple of Witchcraft and author of *City Magick* and *Instant Magick*

"*Divination Conjure Style* is the sort of no-nonsense primer that any student can pick up as a gateway into Southern magical practice, but it also feels like the kind of book that will reward repeated consultation. In a way, Starr Casas is offering you a seat at her table as she riffles her deck of playing cards or throws her bones at your feet. The book is personal—not a conversation exactly—but a chance to hear a voice of wisdom and experience unclouded by distractions (which are all too common in occult writings). Starr's directness never comes off as condescending or dismissive of anyone's experience. Instead, her guidance through divination systems used in Southern-style Conjure is maternal, a hand pointing the way and a voice assuring you that you can do this. She weaves personal stories into her lessons, making the material she covers ring true with a lived authenticity. This book is not a sweeping history of all things Conjure or divinatory—it isn't trying to be that. Instead, Starr writes from her heart and from the well of her experience, and anyone about to pick up a deck of cards, a pendulum, or a pair of bent copper rods can benefit from reading it.

—CORY THOMAS HUTCHESON, cohost of the New World Witchery podcast and author of *54 Devils*

"I was so excited to read Starr Casas's book on divination, and I sure wasn't disappointed! I'm a big lover of all things divination, and though there are tons of books on the tarot, books on other rarer forms of divination are thin on the ground. This magical book gives the reader so much. I learned about forms of divination that I'd never heard of, like blue water reading and egg divination, and all told in such a beautiful, authentic, easygoing, conversational, and dedicated spiritual way. *Divination Conjure Style* is an absolute must for any aspiring reader."

—PATRICIA WESTON, author of *White Witch Patricia Weston's Book of Spells and Magic*

"Divination holds a potent place for the work that spiritualists, witches, rootworkers, and many other magical practitioners do almost on a daily basis. Starr Casas offers a wealth of knowledge when it comes to this particular art. If you want to learn, receive edification, and see just how powerful the art of divination is, I would highly suggest you read *Divination Conjure Style*. Not only is it very detailed, but Starr goes on to explain the whys and not simply the hows. This is a book that covers the spectrum from beginning to end, from an inquisitive mind to the practitioner who has been working divination for decades. This book is a must have for anyone who seeks to learn and increase their knowledge of the art of divination."

—HOODOO SEN MOISE, author of *Working Conjure*

"As of late, I have been hearing and reading a lot about Tarot enthusiasts and their 'Tarot spiritual practice.' However, I have never heard anyone refer to their 'playing cards spiritual practice.' I don't think I've ever even seen a book that combines divination by playing cards and Bible verses. In her book, *Divination Conjure Style*, Starr Casas marries magic (Conjure), divination, and Bible verses. Anyone with a desire to develop a magical and spiritual practice can do so by merely picking up a pack of playing cards, which are very accessible, inexpensive, and nonthreatening. I especially loved the section where she includes other very accessible methods of divination. Having read playing cards myself for over forty years, I was delighted to learn something new!"

—MARY-GRACE FAHRUN, author of *Italian Folk Magic*

"In her landmark new book, *Divination Conjure Style,* Starr Casas provides the depth and breadth of the time-honored tools and skills of divination—the very center post of conjure services, workings, and practices. The undergirding core wisdom that she highlights is how these tap the guidance of the ancestors. Starr immerses the reader in her traditional folk culture, and this ignites every word and concept with life, truth, connection, and the magic to help and heal ourselves, our communities, and those we love. Read, understand, savor, and apply these rare jewels she has given."

—ORION FOXWOOD, author of *The Candle and the Crossroads* and *The Flame in the Cauldron*

Divination
Conjure Style

Divination Conjure Style

Reading Cards, Throwing Bones, *and Other Forms of Household Fortune-Telling*

STARR CASAS

Illustrations by Josef Bailey

Foreword by Judika Illes

WEISER BOOKS

This edition first published in 2019 by Weiser Books, an imprint of
Red Wheel/Weiser, LLC

With offices at:
65 Parker Street, Suite 7
Newburyport, MA 01950
www.redwheelweiser.com

ISBN: 978-1-57863-669-3

Library of Congress Cataloging-in-Publication Data available upon request.

Cover design by Kathryn Sky-Peck
Interior illustrations by Josef Bailey
Interior by Maureen Forys, Happenstance Type-O-Rama
Typeset in Adobe Jenson Pro and IM Fell DW Pica Pro

Printed in Canada
IBI

*To all those who
have gone before us.
We honor you.*

WARNING!

This book contains advice and information on spells and their use. Any reader who uses the spells or any other information within this book does so entirely at their own risk. The author and publisher accept no liability if the spells do not have the desired effect or if adverse effects are caused.

CONTENTS

FOREWORD

Starr Casas is a national treasure. I do not exaggerate. Beyond all her magical and spiritual knowledge, which is vast, she is a testament to a time, not that long ago, but probably before some of you can remember, when American culture was not homogenized; when you'd travel around and hear distinctive music, enjoy local cuisines, and, not least, encounter different magical traditions. A time before every shopping mall in America contained the exact same stores. Consider my own hometown, New York City. Walk down Fifth Avenue today and you might as well be in a mall: same stores, same foods, virtually same everything.

Back in the day, during my youth, New York City had its own distinctive style of magic—a conglomeration of Ceremonial Magick, Wicca, Espiritismo, and more. It was never really written down or documented and is now, I fear, rarely practiced, except perhaps quietly by some old folks. Meanwhile, Starr Casas has found a way of remaining fresh and vital, maintaining her own ancestral, once-regional traditions, updating them as necessary to be relevant to the times, yet always still true to their essence.

When I call Starr a national treasure—perhaps even an *international* treasure—I am being extremely sincere. She is an authentic and self-aware bridge between past, present, and future. Writing this book is her generous gift to anyone interested in Conjure, divination, or American folk culture, whether you are a practitioner or not. But if you, like me, are a practitioner, her gift is priceless.

Children are always asked what they want to be when they grow up. I was an extremely truthful child, or maybe just not smart or savvy enough to know the right answers. My response—that I wished to be a fortune-teller—was inevitably received with stunned silence, which quickly transformed into laughter, as if I must be telling a joke. (I wasn't.) Then the adult would inform me that, in fact, that couldn't possibly be what I desired. No doubt, what I really wanted was to be a teacher, or a doctor, or some other respectable profession.

I had relatives who were passionate card players and so we had plenty of playing card decks in my childhood home. Even then, I knew you could do more than play games with them, although I didn't know how. By the time I was six we had tarot cards, too. But by then I had learned to be discreet about my ambitions. If I had told my mother that I wanted to read cards professionally, she would have taken them away.

Of course, as Lou Reed sings in his song "Sweet Jane," "those were different times." Today there's a glut of instructional books on the market dedicated to divination—including some written specifically for children. But there is no other book like this one, which contains Starr Casas's own techniques, wisdom, and ancestral knowledge. The information in these pages is not something you would ever have previously learned from a book. These skills were not written; you had to be lucky enough to learn them from another person, at least until now.

An underlying theme of this book is that divination does not have to be remote, nor does it have to be prohibitively expensive. Divination is not the exclusive property of the elite, the educated, or the wealthy. It is a basic human skill intended to help us all live our best lives. Magic and tools for divination are everywhere, if only we have the eyes to see and the knowledge to put what we know into practice. Starr teaches us how to do this; to recognize the inherent magical power contained in household items like the family Bible, bones, and plain old playing cards. Crystal balls and ornate pendulums are beautiful, for sure. But the real power is within you, and it can also be accessed via handcrafted pendulums and laundry bluing. Don't worry if this sounds mysterious. In these pages Starr explains all this and more, teaching these skills with plainspoken clarity, so that we can learn to use them regardless of our own personal backgrounds and histories. I feel so blessed to have had the opportunity to learn from Starr Casas and grateful to be able to share these blessings with you.

—JUDIKA ILLES, author of *Encyclopedia of 5,000 Spells* and other books

INTRODUCTION

Divination has always been around, even before biblical times. If you read Ezekiel 21:18–23, God tells Ezekiel that the king of Babylon will cast arrows at the crossroads in front of Jerusalem. In this chapter, God specifically mentions how the arrows tell the king to capture Jerusalem and enslave the Hebrews. It's easy to overlook the fact that God allows this to occur and influences the arrows to do his will:

> *For the king of Babylon stands at the parting of the way, at the head of the two ways, to use divination. He shakes the arrows; he consults the teraphim; he looks at the liver.*
>
> (EZEKIEL 21:21)

You'll even find bone throwing in the Bible. In the Book of Joshua, God authorized Joshua to cast lots (in Conjure we call it "throwing the bones") so the lands around Judea could be divided fairly between seven tribes of Israel:

> *"You are to divide the land into seven parts. Judah is to remain in its territory on the south and the tribes of Joseph in their territory on the north. After you have written descriptions of the seven parts of the land, bring them here to me and I will cast lots for you in the presence of the* Lord *our God."*

> *As the men started on their way to map out the land, Joshua instructed them, "Go and make a survey of the land and write a description of it. Then return to me, and I will cast lots for you here at Shiloh in the presence of the* LORD*."*
>
> (JOSHUA 18:5–6, 18:8)

Divination is a part of God's work and there's nothing evil about it, although some Christians and religious folks may think otherwise. The Old Testament is proof that divination was a big thing: it was used for planting crops, arranging marriages, predicting and helping with births, and discovering who was really right or wrong. Here's one example from Proverbs 16:33:

> *The lot is cast into the lap,*
> *but its every decision is from the* LORD.

And for another example, in Genesis 44, we see that Joseph had a reading cup:

> *When they had gone out of the city, and were not yet far off, Joseph said to his steward, "Get up, follow the men; and when you overtake them, say to them, 'Why have you repaid evil for good?*
>
> *Is not this the one from which my lord drinks, and with which he indeed practices divination? You have done evil in so doing.'"*
>
> (GENESIS 44:4–5)

> *So Judah and his brothers came to Joseph's house, and he was still there; and they fell before him on the ground.*
>
> *And Joseph said to them, "What deed is this you have done? Did you not know that such a man as I can certainly practice divination?"*

> *Then Judah said, "What shall we say to my lord? What shall we speak? Or how shall we clear ourselves? God has found out the iniquity of your servants; here we are my lord's slaves, both we and he also with whom the cup was found."*
>
> (GENESIS 44:14–16)

When you get to the New Testament, though, things get a little tricky. The New Testament claims divination is a sin. How can part of a book be the truth but the other part of the same book be wrong? I think it's that folks fear what they don't know or understand.

I wasn't raised reading cards. I never saw my mama with a deck of cards. We found an old deck when she passed, and I got them, but I would never claim she read them. I learned to read playing cards from my cousin's auntie when we were sixteen. It stuck with me, but my mama did teach me to believe in the Old Testament!

Within these pages I will do my best to share what I know about divination, be it reading the cards, throwing the bones, looking in a glass of blue water, or reading with a pendulum. Any of these tools can be worked with to figure out what is really going on.

Reading with your ancestors and the other spirits that walk with you is a must—that is where the power of a reading comes from! And that is why we begin there. Before you ever pick up a deck of cards or another divination tool, you need to give thanks to the spirits that look out for you and guide your way.

This book might be a little different than others you have read; I am not only a reader but also a Conjure worker. What's a Conjure worker? Conjure workers (also called root workers or two-headed doctors) work with roots, herbs, animal parts, and more to bring about change. They work with both hands, meaning they do what some folks call light and dark works.

You will find works within these pages that deal with right-hand works, and some left-hand works too. The right hand always deals with the blessings and the well wishes; the left hand deals with the harder works, some crossings, and justice works. The ole folks say the right hand should never know what the left hand is doing. Just remember that whichever hand you work with, you and you alone are responsible for your actions!

So there will be Conjure works that may help you reach your goals in life. Even if you are a seasoned reader, there is likely something within these pages that will help you in some way. This is by no means the only way to do divination; this is simply my way! Everyone reads differently and has their own tricks. I'm simply sharing some of mine.

Part One

Preparing Your Tools and Your Space

CALLING ON THE ANCESTORS AND OTHER SPIRITS

The first thing to remember when you are doing divination is that you are opening yourself up not only to the spirits you draw in but also to whatever you or your questioner may have brought in. You need to protect yourself so you don't draw something unwanted into your life. Before I do any consultation, I say a prayer to God, my ancestors, and all the spirits that walk with me for protection and strength. I then ask my ancestors to protect and guide me, and to keep me open and show me the truth while I consult with the client. You never know what may be following someone or what could be attached to them, so this is an important first step.

Before I even start, I have to say that this is just what I have been taught. If you believe something different, that is fine too. I don't think there is one set way to deal with the spirits that walk with us, as we are all different and our spirits are different. It isn't a one-size-fits-all kind of thing. And I write only about spirits and things I work with, so this will in no way be a be-all and end-all list.

We hear folks talk about the spirits that walk with them. What exactly does that mean? Well, I believe these are the spirits that are with us from the time we are conceived in our mother's womb. They are there to help us along the way throughout our lives—to help us navigate situations and be successful and achieve our goals.

I was raised to believe that the spirits are always there to guide me, to uplift me, to protect me, and to show me the directions I should go. By dedicating my cards or other tools to them, I am offering them a way to speak directly to me in a way I can understand. Because spirit can see things that we cannot see. They know things that we do not know. So who better to help us walk in this life that we live?

Now, everyone has an opinion on the ancestors, and you might get a different one from every person you ask. When I say I "work" with my ancestors, I do not mean that I literally send them out and work them. When I am honoring my ancestors and interacting with them, in my world this is considered work.

You can work with more than just your blood kin. Folks come into our lives who mean so much to us they become family. I got into a very heated argument with someone over this many years ago. My sister-in-law, who was also one of my students, got sick and asked me to place her on my ancestor altar should she pass, and I agreed to it. This was about fifteen years ago, and she has been there ever since. I think anyone you have strong feelings for can be placed there.

On the other side of it, you don't necessarily have to work with someone just because they are your kinfolk. Just because someone has passed on doesn't mean they have all of a sudden become this wonderful person. If you had an ancestor who was horrible, you don't have to honor them at all—it is all up to you. Remember that when you are doing spiritual work, you are in charge! (My mama used to say, "A spirit can't hurt you; but it can make you hurt yourself." No matter what you are doing, if you are dealing with spirit you must always stay in control.)

I was taught to believe that any wrong can be righted, any hurt can be mended, and any damage that has been done through the blood can be undone with prayers and petitions. Some may not agree with me, and that is okay; but if it is indeed impossible, as some may think, then our bloodlines would be doomed for past wrongs. That is why I've included a practice for healing past bloodlines, to give you a fresh start.

Most folks say it should be at least a year after someone has passed before they are considered an ancestor. Then again, some folks should not be considered ancestors at all. It really all depends on the person. When my sister-in-law passed, I waited just twenty-one days and then added her photo to my ancestor altar.

You show respect to the ancestors by acknowledging them and the suffering that they went through. By honoring them, I mean lifting their spirits with prayer, a light, smoke, and libation.

Finally, a note of caution. Before you start any type of work, you should call on your God and ancestors to protect you during the work. Once you have called on them for protection, you can call on any other spirit to help in protecting you. This should be done every time you do a reading or stand at your altar.

This may make some folks nervous, but spirits are here to help us, not hinder us. The thing with all spirits is that they can't just step in without being invited. A door must be open for them to step through. Most of the time, these types of spirits want to just hang out. But I have heard stories of spirits running folks and their homes—some to the point that the folks can't rest or live in their own homes anymore. The thing is, something had to have happened—some door was opened—for them to be able to be there. Those are not the spirits that you were born with; those are spirits that have either followed you or may be spirits of place.

If spirits are there to cause havoc, the best way to drive them out is with sulfur. In the old days, folks would say you have to light it and burn it in your home, but sulfur is toxic and should not be burned in closed spaces. I have found over the years that you can simply place it in the corners of a room and it will drive anything unwanted out. (You can learn more about the spirits, ancestors, and spirit work in my other book, *Old Style Conjure*, which goes deeper into these topics.)

SETTING UP AN ANCESTOR ALTAR

If you don't have an altar already, you'll need to set up a small table so you have somewhere to call on your ancestors and to lay out your cards. (I'm sure most already know this, but I'm just throwing this out there because there may be someone reading who has never set up an ancestor altar in their life or doesn't have a clue where to start. So if you already know this information, please forgive me while I explain how to set up for those who may not yet know how.)

When you have decided where you will be placing your altar, you'll need to cleanse the space. Take your wash (see recipe below) and wipe down the wall and the floor where your altar will be. Also wipe off the table really well. Then cleanse the inside and outside of your doors coming into your home. Finally, cleanse your stoop and sidewalk with the remaining wash.

Multipurpose Spiritual Wash/Spray

You will need:

- 3 bay leaves
- 3 olive leaves
- 4 tablespoons baking soda

Making a wash is really nothing more than steeping tea. Add the bay leaves, olive leaves, and baking soda to a gallon of water on the stove. Bring the water to a boil and stir clockwise.

Pray Psalm 23 over the wash three times:

The LORD is my shepherd, I lack nothing.
He makes me lie down in green pastures,
he leads me beside quiet waters,
he refreshes my soul.
He guides me along the right paths
for his name's sake.

Even though I walk
through the darkest valley,
I will fear no evil,
for you are with me;
your rod and your staff,
they comfort me.
You prepare a table before me
in the presence of my enemies.
You anoint my head with oil;
my cup overflows.
Surely your goodness and love will follow me
all the days of my life,
and I will dwell in the house of the Lord
forever.

Then cover the wash with a plate and let it steep.

Once the wash has cooled, it can be put into a spray bottle or a bath, or added to mop water. Save the used bay and olive leaves and place them on each side of your door coming into and out of your home.

Once your table is clean, you need to take at least one cleansing bath before you set up your ancestor altar. (See below.) This may seem like an awful lot of work, but I promise you it will be well worth it in the end.

I have found that when an ancestor altar is set up right, it can be a powerful place. Let me explain. You are setting up this space where your ancestors will sit; not only that, but you are going to be empowering a deck of cards or other tools that you will work with to help you find answers to questions about life and also fix any issues you may run into. Growing up, I was taught that whatever we think of ourselves is how spirit sees us. In other words, we are what we say we are. So if you've been having a bad day, or you just feel beside yourself, you do not want those feelings going into the tools you will be working with to find answers. A cleansing before you start is a must.

Cleansing Bath

First, mix the following ingredients to make a simple bath salt:

- 4 tablespoons table salt
- 4 tablespoons Epsom salts
- 4 tablespoons baking soda

Pour the mixture under warm running water until the tub is full. While you are sitting in the tub, take three deep breaths, letting each one out slowly. Say your petition, asking that whatever is there that shouldn't be there be removed. Then pray Isaiah 41. (You may also pray before or after your bath instead.)

Once you've taken a cleansing bath, you can start working on your altar. Set the altar up to be as elaborate as you would like, but a simple white handkerchief, a cool glass of water, and a white candle will work just fine to start. It all depends on how you want your space to look. Just remember that you have to have room for a glass of water, some candles, and your cards at the very least—so don't make it too crowded. Sometimes less is more.

When you have your table set up, light the candle and then say your prayer and uplifting petitions for the ancestors and invite them to come and sit on your altar. This doesn't take a lot of hocus pocus; simply call on them from your heart and invite them into your home.

DOES ALL THE HOOPLA MATTER?

I've thought about this for many years now: Do we really need all the statues and altar items we all seem to have plenty of in order to honor spirit? As I'm writing, the thought is once again on my mind. Is it all for us, or for spirit? Will spirit still hear us if we don't have a lamp going for them? Will they still shower us with their blessings if we only have our breath and our words? I think that sometimes the need to have all these material things in order to honor spirit is a hindrance.

Before y'all go hollering to the world that I said you don't need these things, though, let me explain.

The work I do was brought over here in the times of slavery. Now do you really think the ancestors were allowed to bring or own such items in such a space? Do you? The answer is no! They were barely allowed to have a set of rags to cover their bodies with and food to stop the hunger pains (notice I didn't say "fill their bellies," because I don't think they got full very often). Let's be truthful for just a moment, please. When Africans were captured and loaded in ships, they had nothing but the spirits that walked with them and the faith that these spirits would get them through it. No statues, no candles, no roots, no curios—absolutely nothing. Yet I'm sure that didn't stop them from praying and petitioning for help.

I'm bringing this up because I think that too many times folks don't do the work because they don't have the money to buy the supplies they are told they "need." In truth, you simply need your breath, your words, and your faith. All the candles, statues, and stuff give you a place to focus, a place to commune with spirit. But in truth you could go to the water's edge or into the woods to commune with the ancestors—and you might even get a stronger message if you did. I am in no way saying that you *shouldn't* have candles, statues, and so on. I have some very special statues where my spirits now sit, and I wouldn't trade them for the world. But I am saying that if you don't have them or can't afford them at the moment and you've got a job to do, don't let that stop you.

Too many times I think we focus too much on material things and not on the ancestors and spirits that walk with us. I truly believe that our ancestors and the spirits that walk with us hear us whether we are simply speaking to them from our hearts or doing some costly work. They are there for us 24-7, and they take us as we come. After all, they chose us! Don't overthink your work, or overprepare with lots of tchotchkes. Just trust in your ancestors and spirit to hear you and make it a success!

HEALING A BLOODLINE

I decided to share some instructions on how I was taught to bring peace to the bloodline of my family. I wasn't going to add this, but I think that folks too many times feel like their bloodline is cursed, either because some worker has told them so or because nothing seems to go right in their lives. Being a professional reader, I have heard this over and over. I'm a firm believer that once that seed is planted, it will continue to grow whether it is true or not.

If I felt there was an issue with my ancestors, I personally would do the following healing before I offered any type of tool for divination. Folks who come in for consultations trust me to be on point and to be able to help them, and I can't do that if I feel my bloodline is cursed.

Bloodline Working

If you believe your bloodline has some corrupt history, then you can offer prayer, libation, petitions, smoke, and light to heal whatever may be there. First, set up your altar. You can place whatever you need to on it, but be sure to include these things:

- A Bible
- A libation of some kind
- A candle
- A source for smoke
- A machete (a pair of scissors will work)

Open your Bible up to Deuteronomy 28. Say your prayers and call for protection. Then present your offerings: the libation, the candle, and the smoke. Cut the air in front of you and around you with the machete/scissors to release the binds that hold your family down.

Pray Deuteronomy 28:1–14, which is a blessing on the bloodline. This is going to be work; nothing is free in life. If you truly believe your bloodline is cursed, then do the work to heal it and your ancestors. Uplift and draw forth the power of your ancestors!

> *And it shall come to pass, if thou shalt hearken diligently unto the voice of the* Lord *thy God, to observe [and] to do all his commandments which I command thee this day, that the* Lord *thy God will set thee on high above all nations of the earth:*
>
> *And all these blessings shall come on thee, and overtake thee, if thou shalt hearken unto the voice of the* Lord *thy God.*
>
> *Blessed thou in the city, and blessed thou in the field.*
>
> *Blessed the fruit of thy body, and the fruit of thy ground, and the fruit of thy cattle, the increase of thy kine, and the flocks of thy sheep.*
>
> *Blessed thy basket and thy store.*
>
> *Blessed thou when thou comest in, and blessed thou when thou goest out.*
>
> *The* Lord *shall cause thine enemies that rise up against thee to be smitten before thy face: they shall come out against thee one way, and flee before thee seven ways.*
>
> *The* Lord *shall command the blessing upon thee in thy storehouses, and in all that thou settest thine hand unto; and he shall bless thee in the land which the* Lord *thy God giveth thee.*
>
> *The* Lord *shall establish thee an holy people unto himself, as he hath sworn unto thee, if thou shalt keep the*

> *commandments of the* LORD *thy God, and walk in his ways.*
>
> *And all people of the earth shall see that thou art called by the name of the* LORD*; and they shall be afraid of thee.*
>
> *And the* LORD *shall make thee plenteous in goods, in the fruit of thy body, and in the fruit of thy cattle, and in the fruit of thy ground, in the land which the* LORD *sware unto thy fathers to give thee.*
>
> *The* LORD *shall open unto thee his good treasure, the heaven to give the rain unto thy land in his season, and to bless all the work of thine hand: and thou shalt lend unto many nations, and thou shalt not borrow.*
>
> *And the* LORD *shall make thee the head, and not the tail; and thou shalt be above only, and thou shalt not be beneath; if that thou hearken unto the commandments of the* LORD *thy God, which I command thee this day, to observe and to do them.*
>
> *And thou shalt not go aside from any of the words which I command thee this day, [to] the right hand, or [to] the left, to go after other gods to serve them.*
>
> (DEUTERONOMY 28:1–14)

Our ancestors are there to help us become more than they were able to become in their own lives. They support us and help us navigate through life. That's why it's so important to set up an altar for them, a place where their spirit can come and sit; a place where they can be honored and uplifted.

We all have different spirits that walk with us; none of us have the same spirits, because we are all different people. Start with your ancestors and move forward from there. Sometimes more is not better;

this is one of those times. Some folks collect spirits to help them like they change their drawers. To me, that is overkill and it weakens the spirits that walk with you. There is no big rush. Take your time, work with your ancestors, and get a feel for the lay of the land. Then move to another helping spirit if you feel the need too. Just don't rush it.

DEDICATING YOUR TOOLS

Anyone can memorize a deck of cards, but there's nothing like being blessed with the gift of sight through your ancestors. When we dedicate our tools to the ancestors or a spirit, we are literally giving them the tools.

What does the word "dedicated" mean? This is what Webopedia has to say:

> *Dedicated means reserved for a specific use. In communications, a dedicated channel is a line reserved exclusively for one type of communication.*

I never thought of my spiritual link with my ancestors as a "dedicated channel," but I guess it is. They come through the bones or the cards to communicate with me. This might not be the "correct" spiritual term, but it explains exactly what happens when you dedicate your tools to the ancestors. That dedication will open up the lines of communication between you and them. You should be able to hear them loud and clear as they speak through your tools, be they cards, bones, candles, etc.

Each worker has his or her own way of dedicating divination tools to the ancestors or spirits. My main divination tools have all been dedicated to my ancestors. I do have some that belong to the spirits that I work with so they can talk to me and give me information, but these are for my personal use only; I do not read for clients with them. Like I said, each reader has their own way of doing things, and my way is by no means the only way. This is just how I was taught to work with divination tools that I will be reading for the public with.

Our ancestors know all and see all. They also have our best interest at heart. This is why our tools should be dedicated to them. They will be the ones that are truly doing the reading; you simply have to discern the information that they are sharing with you. Anyone can memorize something, but to be a truly gifted reader you should be able to hear the spirits speak. By dedicating your reading tools to your ancestors, you are opening up that link. Trust in the power of your ancestors and the spirits that walk with you, and you can never go wrong. Listen to the wisdom they have to share with you.

When I get a new deck of cards or tool, I always cleanse it and give it to my ancestors. Since our ancestors are here to guide us in the right direction, it only makes sense that all divination tools would be given to them or a spirit that walks with you. Spirit always knows much more than we do or ever could—so why not give your cards to your ancestors to fill with their knowledge and their power, so you can see everything that you need to see and even find out things that are hidden?

I'm a firm believer that everything we touch has a spirit on it. Notice I did not say *in* it. Think about the artist who drew that ad you saw in a magazine, or the designer who created the microwave you might be using, or the illustrator for the cards you're using right now. We leave a little bit of our emotions on everything we touch. Even if a deck of cards is brand-new and wrapped in cellophane, someone else had to touch it at some point. How do we know what type of day that person was having? How do we know if they were having loving thoughts or if their whole life was in turmoil? I, for one, don't want someone else's emotions in my spiritual tools. So I cleanse all my tools before working with them.

How exactly do you do this dedication? You call on your ancestors and you petition them to fill your tools with their power so you will be able to understand what they are saying to you. Plain and simple, there is one thing you cannot do in this practice, and that is overthink or analyze it to death. Like the popular shoe commercial says, "Just do it!"

DEDICATION RITUAL

Here is a simple setup for dedicating your tools:

- White handkerchief
- Tools for dedication
- 4 candles

Lay your handkerchief on your ancestor altar and spread your tools on top. Then lay your candles in the shape of a cross around your tools. The first candle goes on the top, the next on the bottom, the next on the right, and the last on the left. (Now, before those who have read my other books can say, "But Starr, you said not to go from left to right unless you are locking something down," wait a minute. That is exactly what you will be doing—locking the power and communication your ancestors share with you into the tools, so they retain that power and insight.)

Light each of the candles in the order you set them down. As you light each candle, call on your ancestors and the spirits that walk with you.

Repeat this process for seven days. On the eighth day, wrap your tools up in their hankie and thank your ancestors. Then give them an offering.

Take your tools and place them in your pillowcase, where you lay your head. Keep them there for seven days. If you have dreams during that time, try to write them down.

After the seven days are up, lay out your handkerchief and hold each tool—be it bones, cards, or a pendulum—up to your mouth and blow three breaths on it. Then say your name three times over it.

Call on God first, and then your ancestors. Petition them to help you understand what is being shown to you, and to communicate with you in a way that you will understand.

Ask a question that you already know the answer to, then use the tool. Sit there quietly for a few minutes. See if you can understand the message.

This is not trickery; you are simply making sure you understand what the ancestors are sharing with you. By blowing your breath over the tool, you are linking your spirit with the one that lives in the tool. When you say your name, the tool knows you are the one the answers are meant for.

CONSULT THE SPIRITS

I learned as a young worker that divination is one of the most important parts of my job; it will save you from a lot of trouble and confusion. It will also let you know what steps you truly need to take or if you should just do nothing. I know sometimes we think that we know what is best for us and we know what it is that we need to do, but this is simply not always true. Sometimes we want something so bad we become blind to what we should be doing. If you don't listen to anything else in this book, remember this: *please make sure that you always do some type of spiritual divination before you move forward with any type of work.* Discernment is the key word here. You really need to learn to listen to your ancestors, because they are the ones that are going to help you understand what the wax is saying or how the candle flame is communicating.

So let's recap. You've established a connection with the spirits that walk with you and your ancestors; you've cleansed your space and created an altar; you've dedicated your tools; and you've consulted the spirits before proceeding with any type of work. You're now ready to open your first reading!

OPENING AND CLOSING A READING

OPENING A READING

The first thing I do when I'm opening a reading is brush myself off or rub myself down with spiritual water (Florida water or some other type of water) or holy oil. This clears my spirit and gets me in the right frame of mind to read.

Here's a recipe for a spiritual water you can make on your own.

Spiritual Water

You will need:

- ½ gallon water
- 3 bay leaves
- 4 tablespoons table salt
- 4 tablespoons Epsom salt

Bring the water to a strong boil and add your ingredients. Let the water boil for three minutes, then turn the fire off and cover the pot. Let it steep until it's cool, then pour the water in a clean glass container.

This water can be added to floor washes, baths, and any general blessings. Bay leaves are powerful; they add protection and power to all works.

Dedicating Your Tools

Next, I assemble my tools:

- White handkerchief
- Solomon's seal root
- 1 red candle
- 1 white candle
- 1 blue candle

When you do a spiritual reading, be it with cards, bones, a pendulum, or a glass of blue water, you need to first call on the Holy Trinity and your ancestors for protection. Then petition the ancestors to fill you with the spirits of discernment so you will know what the truth is and isn't. (I say *spirits* of discernment because I was taught that there are several spirits that walk with us; we simply have to call on them.)

Lay the white hankie out on your reading table. Then hold the red candle up to your mouth and blow three breaths into it. Call on your ancestors and ask them to help you hear the message they are sharing with you. Place the candle on the left side of the handkerchief.

Next, take the white candle and write your name or the client's name in the wax around the wick. Hold the candle up to your mouth and blow three breaths into it. Then dress the candle with some olive oil. Pray that you will be shown whatever you need to see to help your client, and that you will be able to communicate the message in a way they will understand. Then place the white candle to the right of the red one, in the middle of the hankie. If you have a photo of the client, tape it to their candle.

Petition Solomon, the prophet of wisdom. He has a root named after him called Solomon's seal, which promotes wisdom and the gift of knowing what to say and when to say it. Place some Solomon's seal on your reading table as you ask Solomon to help you discern what you need to see. He'll show you the truth for what it is, so you can see the whole picture.

Hold the blue candle up to your mouth. Pray and ask him to fill you with the spirits of discernment. Place the blue candle to the right of the white one, forming a straight line across the hankie.

Next, place your tool on top of the hankie. Then light your candles in the order you set them down as you start your opening prayers. Knock three times on your reading table and petition your ancestors to come and to let only the truth be known in the reading. This is a simple candle setup, but it's a very powerful one! You are opening the door for your ancestors and Solomon to come into the reading and help you understand what you are seeing.

Once you have offered up the tool you will be working with, it's time to call on the spirits of discernment. Hold your tool up to your mouth and pray 1 Kings 3:9–14 over it:

> *"So give your servant a discerning heart to govern your people and to distinguish between right and wrong. For who is able to govern this great people of yours?"*
>
> *The Lord was pleased that Solomon had asked for this. So God said to him, "Since you have asked for this and not for long life or wealth for yourself, nor have asked for the death of your enemies but for discernment in administering justice, I will do what you have asked. I will give you a wise and discerning heart, so that there will never have been anyone like you, nor will there ever be. Moreover, I will give you what you have not asked for—both wealth and honor—so that in your lifetime you will have no equal among kings. And if you walk in obedience to me and keep my decrees and commands as David your father did, I will give you a long life."*

When you are finished praying, it is time to start the reading. If you are reading for a client or yourself, the steps are the same.

It is very important that you know how to open and close the gate to the spirits. I was taught that just the act of laying out the cards or throwing the bones is opening the door for spirits to walk through, so you need to know how to shut that door once it is open.

CLOSING A READING

Anytime you light a candle and start to pray, you open a door. When you are finished with your work, that door needs to be closed. For me, the closing is just as important as the opening; you don't want a spirit that might have been drawn to the reading hanging around after the consultation is over.

When the reading is over, give thanks and honor to your ancestors, Solomon, and the spirits of discernment. Pick up your tool and hold it to your mouth. Blow three strong breaths over it and say, "Ancestors, I petition you. Just as you woke this tool up, will you now put it back to sleep until I call on you again?"

Thank your higher power and your ancestors for showing you the way. Then call on Solomon and thank him for sharing his wisdom with you during the reading. Let the candles burn out as an offering to the spirits.

You should also get in the habit of brushing yourself off after each reading. When you do spiritual readings for folks, you open your spirit up in order to understand what spirit is trying to communicate. When you open up during a reading, you will pull some of the other person's mess onto yourself. Clean it off so it doesn't affect you or your next reading.

I believe that our breath holds our spirit and that it can attach itself to the bones if they are not cleansed. We have to remember that not everyone has a clean spirit, and I personally do not want someone else's issues following me home. So you should always cleanse your divination tools, whether it be the bones, cards, pendulum, or whatever you are working with. You can cleanse your tool by scratching it with a chicken foot, blowing three breaths over it, or passing it through smoke.

Part Two

Card Divination

GETTING STARTED

Playing cards are a specialty of old-timey Conjure workers and spiritual readers, and they have a special meaning to Conjure workers and gifted readers alike. In traditional Conjure work, there are special meanings and works for the playing cards that you won't find elsewhere. In fact, the playing cards are a work in themselves. In Conjure, when you work with the playing cards you can reverse the outcome revealed in that card. There are special setups and prayers you can work with to better your circumstances and remove any blocks that come in your life. For example, if you see blocks when dealing the deals, there are road opening works you can do.

Playing cards tell a story. As the reader, you only need to let spirit open your eyes so that you can discern the story and see how it applies to your life or the life of the person you are reading for. Some people feel there are drawbacks to reading the playing cards because there are no pictures (like in tarot cards) and you have to memorize the numbers. I disagree; because anytime you are doing a reading, you are opening yourself up to spirit. Spirit is the one giving you the information to help you or your client in need. If you are open to spirit and have a strong relationship with your ancestors, then you will know what the spirits are saying—whether you're reading the playing cards, throwing the bones, or looking into a jar of blue water. You have to trust in God or your higher power and let the spirit guide you if you want to be a good reader.

CLEANSING THE DECK

Open your new deck of cards and shuffle them a few times just to mix them up and so you can get the feel of them. Make a note of how the cards feel, your impression of them. By doing this, you'll be able to really notice the difference in the way they feel after they are cleansed. Then go to your ancestor altar and spread them out faceup. You don't know who has touched these cards, and what type of emotional feelings they have left on them. So these cards truly need to be spiritually cleansed before you start working with them.

To start, create your sulfur mixture. (See below.) You will also need:

- 5 pieces of parchment paper or a brown paper bag
- 5 stick candles or tea lights
- 3 red seven-day candles
- Your deck of cards

Sulfur Mix

You can't use spiritual washes or sprays or any of that stuff on a deck of cards. So how exactly do you cleanse them? You have to remember that I come from the old days, when folks used sulfur, turpentine, castor oil, and other things that we now know are not good for us.

I still cleanse my cards the old way I was taught to, using a mixture of sulfur and salt. Nowadays it is kind of hard to find, but most feed stores will have it under the name "garden sulfur." It's not the powdered sulfur—it's made into pellets—but it still works. As times change, we have to adapt to those changes. And this happens to be one of those times.

To be clear: *You should never burn sulfur in your home.* Just placing it in the corners of a room or on an altar is good enough.

Using gloves, mix 3 tablespoons salt and 3 tablespoons sulfur in a bowl. Spread the mix around the corners of your house or place on your altar, as needed.

Cleansing Working

When I was young, I was taught to work with stick candles. If you really want to do it the way I was taught, then you need stick candles instead of tea lights. However, if you are going to burn stick candles, then you need to put your sulfur mixture under the candleholder—because if the fire from the stick candle reaches that sulfur, it will set the sulfur on fire. This is why tea lights work much better. I know a lot of folks nowadays think that working with tea lights is antispiritual or something, but they make works easier. You're really not taking away from tradition, because you're still working with traditional ingredients.

You also need three red seven-day candles that you are going to place on the back side of the table. These represent the Holy Trinity and the blood of the ancestors. You will light going from right to left because you want to open the altar up for the ancestors to be able to come in.

Set your pieces of parchment paper around your cards in this order: top, bottom, right, left. Then put a pinch of your sulfur mixture on top of each piece of paper in the same order you laid them down. Place a tea light on top of your ingredients in the same way.

Take the last paper and ingredients and place it on top of your cards in the center. Light the center candle first, then light the rest in the same order you set them down: top, bottom, right, left. Let the candles burn until they go out. While they are burning, petition your ancestors to cleanse away anything that is not meant to be on the cards.

Repeat the candle burns daily until your red candles have burned completely out. Then move on to the next step of the work.

Once the red candles burn out, discard the sulfur mixture. Clean up your altar and set down a fresh glass of cool water and light a white candle. Then place your cards back on the altar. Give honor and thanks to your ancestors as the candle burns. Offer up prayers for them, tell them how much they mean to you. Lift them up!

Then pick up your cards, hold them in your hands, and relax a minute. Remember how the cards felt before they were cleansed? You should be able to feel a big difference in them now. Shuffle the cards and work them for a little while. Then place them on your altar. Let the candle burn completely out before starting the next step.

Every day, as the candle is burning, offer up prayers for your ancestors. Also shuffle your cards and get to know them during this time.

Once your offering candle has burned out, it is time to petition your ancestors to fill your cards with discernment and knowledge. Once again, shuffle your cards well and hold them in your hands for a few minutes. Write down in your log what they feel like. This is so you will be able to feel the difference from when you first open your cards up until this point. Set the cards down and spread them out.

Place five white seven-day candles in this order: one on the top, one in the center, one on the bottom, one on the left, one on the right. (I'm sure you noticed that we are going left to right because we want to nail down this power work and hold it within the cards.)

Starting at the top, light the first candle and call on your ancestors. Ask them to come and sit on your cards so that you will have the wisdom and the knowledge that they wish to share through the cards. Say the same petition as you light each of your candles in order. Repeat your petition daily until the candles have all burned out.

While you are working the altar, you can also petition your ancestors to bless you with some holy oil that you dress yourself with before reading. (See recipe below.)

Holy Oil

Just as it's good to have some sulfur mix to cleanse your space, it's also good to have a bottle of holy oil around to bless yourself and pieces of your altar.

You will need:

- 1 cinnamon stick
- Pinch of calamus

- 3 bay leaves
- New bottle of olive oil

Add the cinnamon, calamus, and bay leaves to the olive oil and place it, uncapped, on your altar. Keep the oil in the setup for seven days.

The best time to start this is when the hands of the clock are moving upward and the sun is high in the sky.

Once the seven days are up, you can use it to dress candles, rub on your hands before a card reading, address your third eye, and address the crown of your head so that you're protected during a reading.

Surround your holy oil with tea lights, placing them in this order: top, bottom, left, right. Once again, go left to right in order to nail down the power that your ancestors are going to fill your holy oil with. Light the candles in the way you laid them out. As you light each candle, call on your ancestors to fill that holy oil with their power so that you may always be protected, have the gift of discernment, and understand what they are trying to tell you.

Once the candles have burned out, shuffle your cards well, hold them up to your mouth, and say your name over them three times. Then blow three breaths on the cards. When you are finished, wrap your cards in a white handkerchief. (You'll store your cards like this anytime you are not working with them.) For seven days, sleep with your cards inside your pillow. Now your cards are ready to work with.

I know this may seem like a lot of work, but it is well worth it and I think you will see a difference in how your cards read for you and the amount of information you can draw from them in a reading. Keep notes on your readings for a while so you can see the difference in the cards. The more you work the cards, the stronger the bond will become between y'all.

CARD READING BASICS

I know many folks already know how to read playing cards, but there is always some new little trick that we can learn. I want to share some of my secrets with you, things that I have not written about or shared before, like working with the prophet Elijah for justice, or with Saint Peter to draw in success and prosperity.

You will find in the chapter that follows card **meanings** and card **actions**. This is where your ancestors and the spirits that walk with you come in. It is important that you learn to listen to them, so you will have the spirits of discernment with you during your consultation or readings, so you know which message applies to this card.

You will also find corresponding **Bible verses** that can be prayed over the card in a work to help you with any situation. These are by no means the only verses that could be prayed over the cards, but they are the ones I work with and have found to be successful. The verse is there as further insight into the particular card but may also be used as a form of bibliomancy. In other words, if you don't have a Bible but you do have a deck of playing cards, you can pick a card to discover a relevant passage.

I'll give a couple examples of how this works. Let's start with the king of hearts.

SAMPLE READING: KING OF HEARTS

Most folks know that the king of hearts represents a man with light features. But what else is there to know? Sometimes a card can also tell us—or warn us, I should say—about the actions of another. The king of hearts is one of those cards.

> *Meaning: A good-hearted man but very rash in his judgments. Don't rely on him for good advice. He is very generous but prone to gossip.*
>
> *Action: Don't share your innermost secrets with him. Perform a clearing work like the one described below.*
>
> *For I am afraid that when I come I may not find you as I want you to be, and you may not find me as you want me*

> *to be. I fear that there may be discord, jealousy, fits of rage, selfish ambition, slander, gossip, arrogance and disorder.*
> (2 CORINTHIANS 12:20)

As we can see, this fellow is basically a good guy, but he loves to gossip and can't hold water, as the ole folks say. This doesn't make him a bad person; it simply means that he can't keep his mouth shut. If you find yourself dealing with such a person, you can do the next work to shut his mouth.

Work for Handling a Gossip

Set up a small altar, and gather the following items:

- A Bible
- A photo of the target (the person you are working on)
- King of hearts
- 1 red candle
- 3 white candles

Open the Bible to 2 Corinthians 12:20. Place the photo of the gossip on the altar, then cover it with the king of hearts.

Take the red candle, and with a marker make a mouth on the glass. Write the target's name in the mouth, then make three *X*'s over the mouth. Write the target's name inside the wax of the candle next to the wick, then pray 2 Corinthians 12:20 into the candle. Place this candle over the target and the card.

Next, pray your petition for peace and for the gossip to stop. In the wax of each white candle, write the target's name next to the wick. On top of the name write the words "Peace be still." It doesn't matter if you can read it or not—spirit knows it is there. Then place one candle at the top, above the red candle, one to the left, and the other one to the right, forming a triangle.

Light your red candle first and pray 2 Corinthians 12:20 over the candle three times. On every line call out the target's name and tell them to stop gossiping about you. Claim there will be peace.

Then light your white candles as you set them down: top, left, and right. As you light each candle, call the target's name out and say, "Peace be still." Do this three times per candle.

Repeat the prayers and petitions daily. It may take a while, but keep pushing until your target learns to keep their lips shut!

SAMPLE READING: TEN OF DIAMONDS

> *Meaning: Success in reference to your question. Total success, money, love, joy.*
>
> *Action: Perform the crown of success work below.*
>
> *Bible verse: In this way the man grew exceedingly prosperous and came to own large flocks, and female and male servants, and camels and donkeys.*
>
> (GENESIS 30:43)

Crown of Success Work

When I do crown of success work I like to use a deep yellow or gold candle, but you can do the work with the color of your choosing.

You will need:

- A Bible
- A photo of the target
- Ten of diamonds
- 5 yellow candles

Set up a small altar and open the Bible to Genesis 30:43. Place the photo of the target on the table and cover it with the ten of diamonds.

Write the target's name around the wick of all five candles. Then write "Crowned with Success" over their name.

Blow three breaths and pray your petition into each candle. Then set one candle on the card, then one at the top, one at the bottom, one to the right, and one to the left. Pray again over the center candle, then over each of the other candles you laid down. Always go in the order that you lay the candles out.

Once you have all the candles lit, pray Genesis 30:43 over the work three times per candle and call the target's name out on each line, claiming total success for them:

> *In this way the man grew exceedingly prosperous and came to own large flocks, and female and male servants, and camels and donkeys.*

Keep the work going until the candles go out or the target is crowned with the success they are looking for.

CARD READING Q&A

Q: How do I choose the right deck?

A: I feel like the right deck will choose you and you will be very drawn to it. There will be something about the cards that makes you want to have them.

Q: Do I always have to cleanse the deck?

A: Yes, you do need to cleanse your deck or any tool that you work with before you do your first reading. The cards are a spiritual tool and you don't know who has handled them or what kinds of emotions the cards have absorbed. As I was taught, every tool must have a bond with whoever is working with it, and in order to do that it needs to be cleansed and fresh.

Q: What are some other ways to cleanse a new deck besides the main ritual you talked about earlier?

A: There are many different ways to cleanse your deck. A word of advice, though: do not spray your deck with any type of spiritual water, because that will mess the cards up. You can smoke your deck to remove any emotions that the deck might have picked up. You can also set the cards in a container of salt and leave them there for at least twenty-four hours. But the best way that I personally have found to cut and clear a deck or any new divination tool is to place it on my ancestor altar and petition my ancestors to clear away anything that has been attached to the deck so it will always read true.

It's important that you cleanse your tools before you work with them because you don't know who has handled them or what their mood was. Remember that these decks are made by companies. What if the person who was working on the line making your deck that day was in a bad mood or had a cross condition on them? You wouldn't want that pulled into your spiritual life. So clean your deck!

Q: How do you connect with your deck of cards?

A: It's important that you connect with your deck of cards so you will be able to discern what it is they're trying to tell you during a reading. The longer you work with a deck, the stronger the bond between you and that deck will become. Once you cleanse your deck, wrap it in a white handkerchief and place it in your pillowcase. Sleep with the deck every night for at least twenty-one days. Take the deck out as much as possible and interact with it. The more you come in contact with your deck, the stronger your bond will become and the sooner you will be in sync. Some folks carry their decks against their skin during the day so they will be close to their spirit.

Q: Does the client need to touch the cards?

A: I don't think that it is necessary for a client to touch or shuffle the cards before reading. I have found that I can read for folks regardless of whether they are with physically with me or talking to me over the phone.

Q: What is the difference between reading the card upright and reverse?

A: Most of the time, when I lay out the cards I read them starting in the upper right direction. But there are times when I will look at them in reverse if I am reading about a certain situation. If a card is laid out in the upright position, I take that to mean that the card means exactly what it is saying. If a card is turned in the reverse position, then that tells me it will either be worse or better, depending on the card that is pulled.

Q: Should you let others read with your deck?

A: I personally would never let anyone read with my deck. My cards are connected to my spirit, and just like I wouldn't let anyone handle my spirit, I'm not going to let them handle my cards that have bonded with my spirit. Some folks might not agree with this, and that's okay. But I'm very superstitious, and so I'm not going to open the door for someone to connect with my spirit through my cards.

Q: How should I store my deck?

A: Your cards should be treated with the utmost respect, so when you are not working with them, they should be wrapped in a white handkerchief or some other type of cloth and put away. They can be stored in a nice card box or be placed in a drawer where they will be safe. They should never be strewn all over the place, as that is disrespectful to the spirit within the cards and the spirits that walk with you.

Q: Can I read in my bed?

A: I personally would not advise reading in bed. When you do spiritual readings, you open yourself up to spirit to communicate with you through the cards. Therefore, you are pulling spirits into the place where you lay down and sleep at night. When you are asleep, you are defenseless. Why would you open the door for some spirits to come in and nest in your bed when you are asleep and defenseless? It may seem like reading cards is not dangerous, but it is if you are opening yourself up to spirits and then not closing that door.

Q: How do you dispose of a deck of cards?

A: If you have an old deck of cards or a new deck that you just cannot deal with, do not throw them in the trash. That is very disrespectful. The best way to dispose of them is to either burn them and spread their ashes or wrap them up nicely and bury them under a tree (preferably an oak, as it has the power to absorb).

You should have a good idea on how to work with the prayers and cards to meet your needs. There will be works throughout this book that are aimed to help you achieve your goals and to help you in your daily life. Now on to the cards!

HEARTS

ACE OF HEARTS

Meaning: Good news, love, happiness. Your troubles and problems are moving away from you.

Action: You are growing strong emotionally and spiritually. Embrace this change.

Bible verse:

> *And He will make you high above all nations which He has made, in praise and in fame and in honor, and that you shall be a holy people to the Lord your God, as He has spoken.*
>
> (DEUTERONOMY 26:19)

KING OF HEARTS

Meaning: A good-hearted man but very rash in his judgments. Don't rely on him for good advice. He is very generous, but prone to gossip.

Action: Don't share your innermost secrets with him. Perform a clearing work.

Bible verse:

> *For I am afraid that when I come I may not find you as I want you to be, and you may not find me as you want me to be. I fear that there may be discord, jealousy, fits of rage, selfish ambition, slander, gossip, arrogance and disorder.*
>
> (2 CORINTHIANS 12:20)

QUEEN OF HEARTS

Meaning: A kind, loving, wise woman who will give you good advice. A very intuitive woman.

Action: Changes take place within your spirit to allow spiritual growth. Accept the change.

Bible verse:

> *How delightful is your love, my sister, my bride!*
>
> *How much more pleasing is your love than wine, and the fragrance of your perfume more than any spice!*
>
> *Your lips drop sweetness as the honeycomb, my bride;*
>
> *milk and honey are under your tongue.*
>
> (SONG OF SONGS 4:10–11)

JACK OF HEARTS

Meaning: The other cards around this one are an indication of the person's intent. This card also represents the inquirer's best friend.

Action: Now is the time for emotional renewal. Take a set of five cleansing baths.

Bible verse:

> *Do not be conformed to this world, but be transformed by the renewal of your mind, that by testing you may discern what is the will of God, what is good and acceptable and perfect.*
>
> (ROMANS 12:2)

TEN OF HEARTS

Meaning: Good luck, success. This is an important card. It counteracts any bad cards that are next to it.

Action: The roads are opened and good things are on the way. Be on the lookout for them.

Bible verse:

> *So now faith, hope, and love abide, these three; but the greatest of these is love.*
>
> (1 CORINTHIANS 13:13)

NINE OF HEARTS

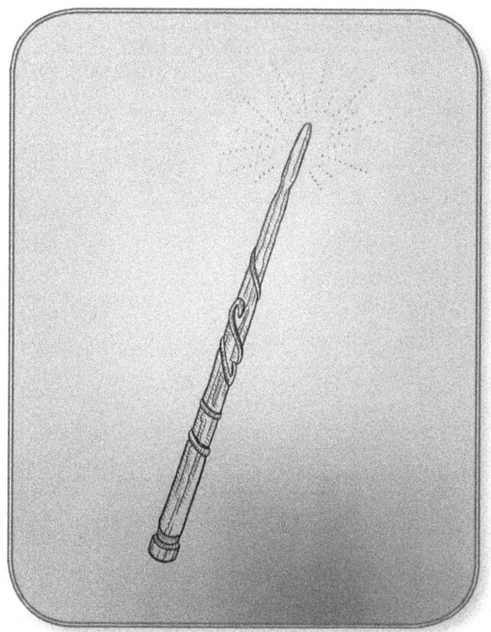

Meaning: This is the card of satisfaction; the wish card. All your dreams and desires will come true.

Action: Good fortune is on the way after a difficult time financially—celebrate it.

Bible verse:

> *And they shall build houses, and inhabit them; and they shall plant vineyards, and eat the fruit of them.*
>
> *They shall not build, and another inhabit; they shall not plant, and another eat: for as the days of a tree are the days of my people, and mine elect shall long enjoy the work of their hands.*

They shall not labour in vain, nor bring forth for trouble; for they are the seed of the blessed of the Lord, *and their offspring with them.*

(ISAIAH 65:21–23)

EIGHT OF HEARTS

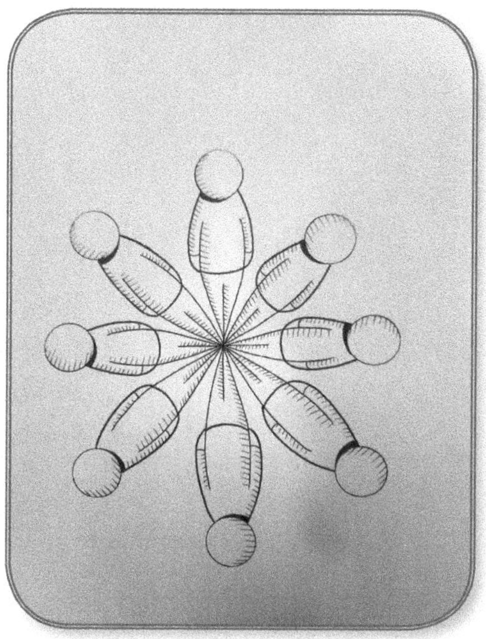

Meaning: This is the card of movement. Things will finally move in the direction you want them to.

Action: You have decided to leave the situation you are in and move forward.

Bible verse:

> *By faith Abraham, when called to go to a place he would later receive as his inheritance, obeyed and went, even though he did not know where he was going. By faith he made his home in the promised land like a stranger in a foreign country; he lived in tents, as did Isaac and Jacob, who were heirs with him of the same promise. For he was looking forward to the city with foundations, whose architect and builder is God.*
>
> (HEBREWS 11:8–10)

SEVEN OF HEARTS

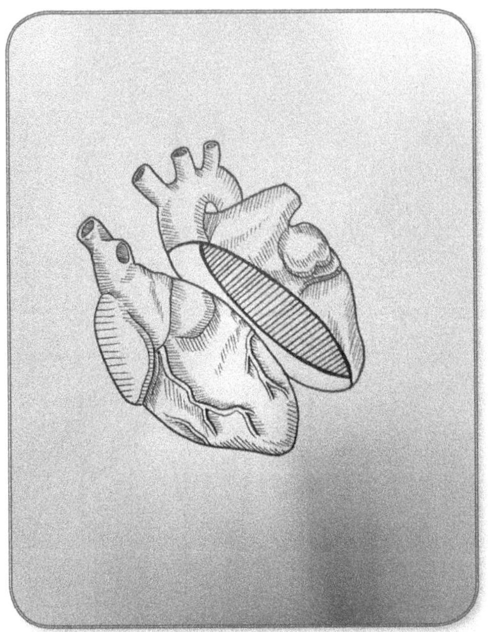

Meaning: This card represents total confusion. Someone who's unreliable, more an enemy than a friend.

Action: It's time to do a cut and clear to remove yourself from the person or situation. Take a cleansing bath each day for seven consecutive days.

Bible verse:

> *Happy is the man who finds skillful and godly Wisdom, and the man who gets understanding, For the gaining of it is better than the gaining of silver, and the profit of it better than fine gold. Skillful and godly Wisdom is more precious than rubies; and nothing you can wish for is to be compared to her. Length of days is in her right hand, and in her left hand are riches and honor.*
>
> (PROVERBS 3:13–17)

SIX OF HEARTS

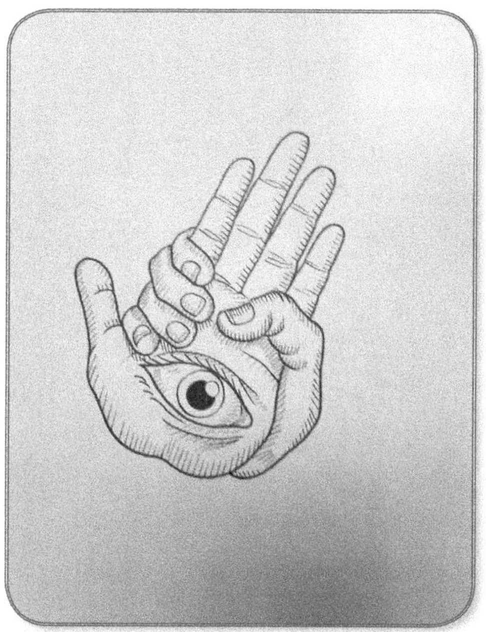

Meaning: It's time to let go of the past so you can move forward. If you have spades around this card, someone is trying to swindle you.

Action: Let go of the anger. You are closing your own roads. Watch out for untrustworthy people.

Bible verse:

> *"For You are my lamp, O LORD; the LORD shall enlighten my darkness. For by You I can run against a troop; by my God I can leap over a wall. As for God, His way is perfect; the word of the LORD is proven; He is a shield to all who trust in Him."*
>
> (2 SAMUEL 22:29–31)

FIVE OF HEARTS

Meaning: All movement has stopped. You are in a rut, and depression has set in. You are unable to make a decision, because you are confused. You are being hit with jealousy and ill will from people around you.

Action: If you pull this card, you need to do some cleansing work.

Bible verse:

> *He has walled me in so I cannot escape;*
> *he has weighed me down with chains.*
> *Even when I call out or cry for help,*
> *he shuts out my prayer.*
> *He has barred my way with blocks of stone;*
> *he has made my paths crooked.*
>
> (LAMENTATIONS 3:7–9)

FOUR OF HEARTS

Meaning: Postponements, delays. A change in the home or at work.

Action: You have built walls around your heart and refuse to let changes come through. Change is coming; be open to it.

Bible verse:

> *But they that wait upon the* Lord *shall renew their strength; they shall mount up with wings as eagles; they shall run, and not be weary; and they shall walk, and not faint.*
>
> (ISAIAH 40:31)

THREE OF HEARTS

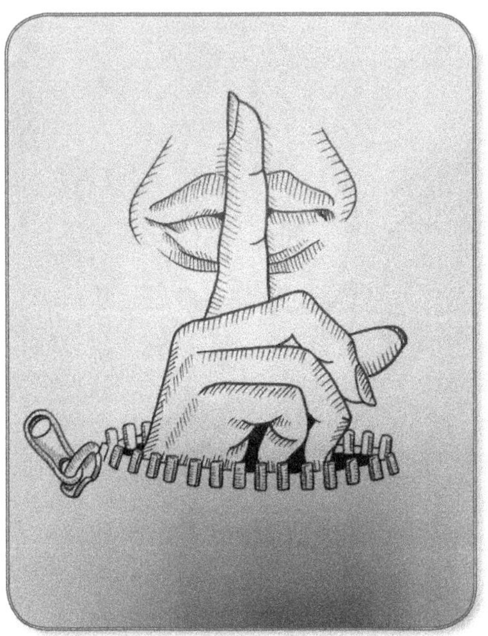

Meaning: Confusion; inability to make a clear decision. Emotional problems.

Action: Be cautious; don't make impulsive decisions or jump into anything. Keep your mouth shut.

Bible verse:

> *For wisdom will enter your heart,*
> *and knowledge will be pleasant to your soul.*
> *Discretion will protect you,*
> *and understanding will guard you.*
>
> (PROVERBS 2:10–11)

TWO OF HEARTS

Meaning: Prosperity and success are yours. Notice the surrounding cards.

Action: Give careful thought about changing jobs. If this card falls next to spades, then do some road opening work.

Bible verse:

> *This Book of the Law shall not depart out of your mouth, but you shall meditate on it day and night, that you may observe and do according to all that is written in it. For then you shall make your way prosperous, and then you shall deal wisely and have good success.*
>
> (JOSHUA 1:8)

DIAMONDS

ACE OF DIAMONDS

Meaning: Happiness, prosperity. Roads are opened. Profitable opportunities await. Rewards for hard work.

Action: The job is yours. Now is the time to follow your dreams.

Bible verse:

> *Then the Lord reached out his hand and touched my mouth and said to me, "I have put my words in your mouth. See, today I appoint you over nations and kingdoms to uproot and tear down, to destroy and overthrow, to build and to plant."*
>
> (JEREMIAH 1:9–10)

KING OF DIAMONDS

Meaning: A fair-haired man; stubborn, vindictive, powerful, and dangerous when crossed. Career achievements.

Action: Your roads are opened; proceed faster. You are moving in the right direction. Do not divert from your path.

Bible verse:

> *"He does not take his eyes off the righteous;*
> *he enthrones them with kings*
> *and exalts them forever.*
> *But if people are bound in chains,*
> *held fast by cords of affliction,*
> *he tells them what they have done—*
> *that they have sinned arrogantly.*
> *He makes them listen to correction*

and commands them to repent of their evil.
If they obey and serve him,
they will spend the rest of their days in prosperity
and their years in contentment."

(JOB 36:7–11)

QUEEN OF DIAMONDS

Meaning: A fair-haired woman, she is a busybody and interferes in others' affairs.

Action: No need for changes; you are set on the right course.

Bible verse:

> *Remember this: Whoever sows sparingly will also reap sparingly, and whoever sows generously will also reap generously. Each of you should give what you have decided in your heart to give, not reluctantly or under compulsion, for God loves a cheerful giver. And God is able to bless you abundantly, so that in all things at all times, having all that you need, you will abound in every good work.*
>
> (2 CORINTHIANS 9:6–8)

JACK OF DIAMONDS

Meaning: A person who is not really reliable. They are selfish or jealous. Bad news. They put themselves first.

Action: You are on the top of your game; the world can be yours.

Bible verse:

> *"Your father's blessings are greater*
> *than the blessings of the ancient mountains,*
> *than the bounty of the age-old hills.*
> *Let all these rest on the head of Joseph,*
> *on the brow of the prince among his brothers."*
>
> (GENESIS 49:26)

TEN OF DIAMONDS

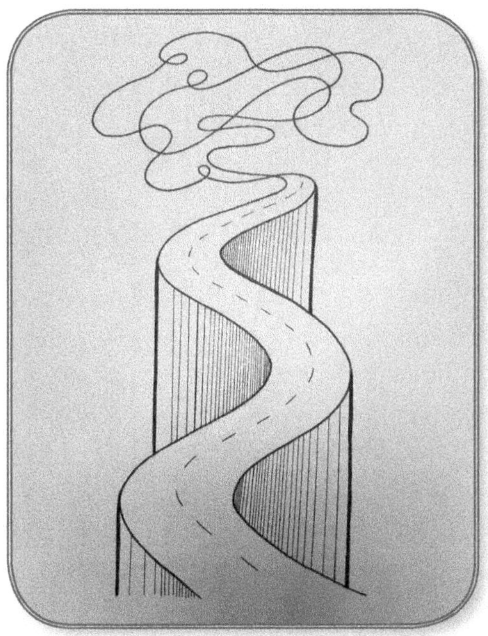

Meaning: Success in reference to your question. Total success, money, love, joy.

Action: Perform the Crown of Success work.

Bible verse:

> *In this way the man grew exceedingly prosperous and came to own large flocks, and female and male servants, and camels and donkeys.*
>
> (GENESIS 30:43)

NINE OF DIAMONDS

Meaning: Opportunities arise.

Action: It's your time for success. Don't go into partnerships; you will do better acting on your own.

Bible verse:

> *I urge you, brothers and sisters, to watch out for those who cause divisions and put obstacles in your way that are contrary to the teaching you have learned. Keep away from them. For such people are not serving our Lord Christ, but their own appetites. By smooth talk and flattery they deceive the minds of naive people. Everyone has heard about your obedience, so I rejoice because of you; but I want you to be wise about what is good, and innocent about what is evil.*
>
> (ROMANS 16:17–19)

EIGHT OF DIAMONDS

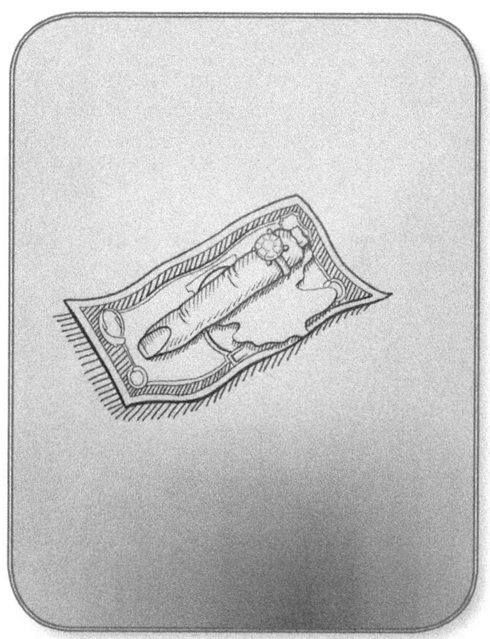

Meaning: Hard work brings success and money.

Action: You will have success. Keep your eyes on your goal to maintain the best results. Don't get sidetracked.

Bible verse:

> *You may say to yourself, "My power and the strength of my hands have produced this wealth for me." But remember the* Lord *your God, for it is he who gives you the ability to produce wealth, and so confirms his covenant, which he swore to your ancestors, as it is today.*
>
> (DEUTERONOMY 8:17–18)

SEVEN OF DIAMONDS

Meaning: Lies, gossip, unlucky gambler, criticism. Overspending.

Action: Take a set of five cleansing baths and do some road opening work.

Bible verse:

> *Wealth gained hastily will dwindle,*
> *but whoever gathers little by little will increase it.*
>
> (PROVERBS 13:11)

SIX OF DIAMONDS

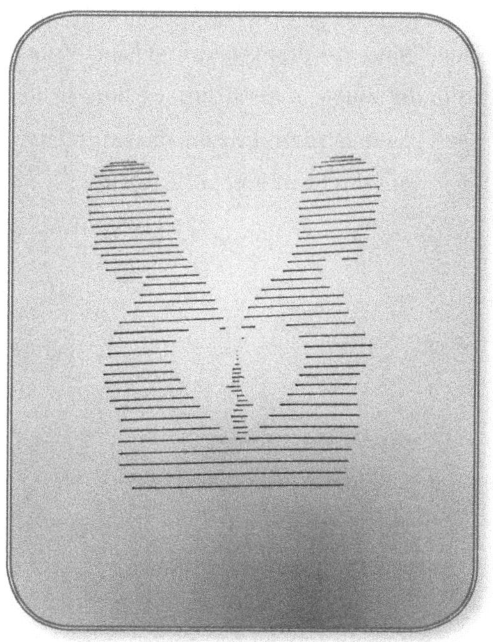

Meaning: A reconciliation. A lost love returns or a rift is mended. Possibly a gift of money.

Action: You must open yourself up in order to receive the gifts offered to you.

Bible verse:

> *"I will make peace your governor*
> *and well-being your ruler.*
> *No longer will violence be heard in your land,*
> *nor ruin or destruction within your borders,*
> *but you will call your walls Salvation*
> *and your gates Praise."*
>
> (ISAIAH 60:17–18)

Or

> *And Azariah the chief priest, from the family of Zadok, answered, "Since the people began to bring their contributions to the temple of the* Lord, *we have had enough to eat and plenty to spare, because the* Lord *has blessed his people, and this great amount is left over."*
>
> (2 CHRONICLES 31:10)

FIVE OF DIAMONDS

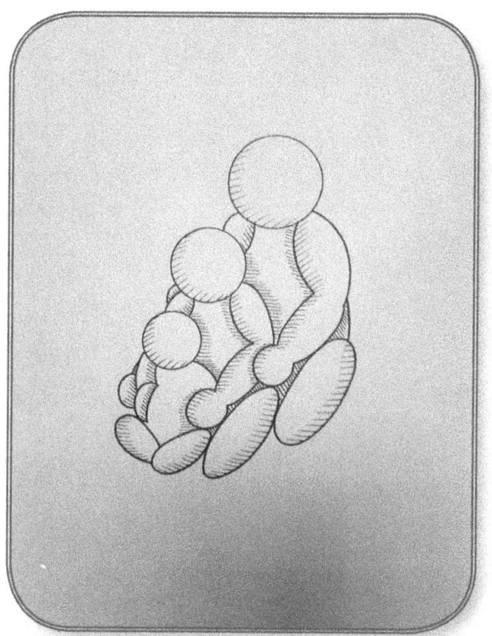

Meaning: Unexpected news, or success in business enterprises. A happy family.

Action: You are miserable. Be grateful for your blessings and stop worrying about what you don't have.

Bible verse:

> *"Be strong and very courageous. Be careful to obey all the law my servant Moses gave you; do not turn from it to the right or to the left, that you may be successful wherever you go. Keep this Book of the Law always on your lips; meditate on it day and night, so that you may be careful to do everything written in it. Then you will be prosperous and successful. Have I not commanded*

you? Be strong and courageous. Do not be afraid; do not be discouraged, for the Lord *your God will be with you wherever you go."*

(JOSHUA 1:7–9)

FOUR OF DIAMONDS

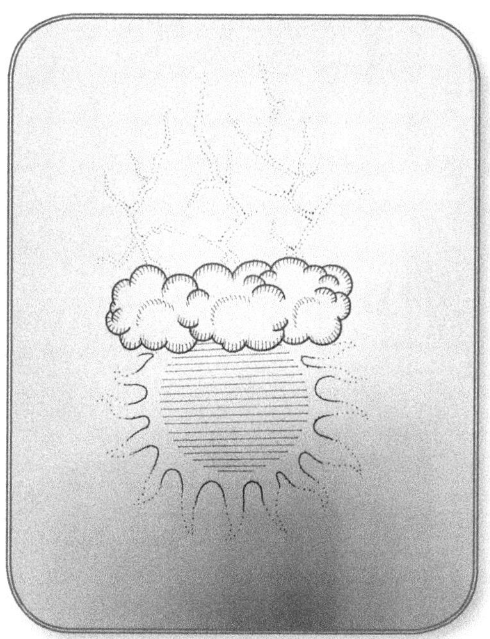

Meaning: Clinging to the past.

Action: You are blocking yourself. Release the fear that is binding you. Do a cut and clear and a road opening.

Bible verse:

> *"Be strong and courageous. Do not fear or be in dread of them, for it is the* Lord *your God who goes with you. He will not leave you or forsake you."*
>
> (DEUTERONOMY 31:6)

THREE OF DIAMONDS

Meaning: Quarrels; domestic disagreements.

Action: You need to keep a cool head. Do a peaceful home vigil tonight.

Bible verse:

> *Two are better than one,*
> *because they have a good return for their labor:*
> *If either of them falls down,*
> *one can help the other up.*
> *But pity anyone who falls*
> *and has no one to help them up.*
> *Also, if two lie down together, they will keep warm.*
> *But how can one keep warm alone?*
> *Though one may be overpowered,*
> *two can defend themselves.*
> *A cord of three strands is not quickly broken.*
>
> (ECCLESIASTES 4:9–12)

TWO OF DIAMONDS

Meaning: Indecisive; noncommittal.

Action: You are having trouble making a commitment. Your indecisiveness could cause long-term problems. You must decide to commit in order to find fulfillment in your life.

Bible verse:

> *"So is my word that goes out from my mouth:*
> *It will not return to me empty,*
> *but will accomplish what I desire*
> *and achieve the purpose for which I sent it.*
> *You will go out in joy*
> *and be led forth in peace."*
>
> (ISAIAH 55:11–12)

CLUBS

ACE OF CLUBS

Meaning: Harmony, achievements, love, peace of mind, professional success, peaceful home, progress, and success.

Action: You are the only one who can hold yourself back. It's time to act.

Bible verse:

> *The fruit of righteousness will be peace; the effect of righteousness will be quietness and confidence forever. My people will live in peaceful dwelling places, in secure homes, in undisturbed places of rest.*
>
> (ISAIAH 32:17–18)

KING OF CLUBS

Meaning: A dark-haired man who is honest, open, and faithful. He is true in his affections.

Action: You have new ideas and the ability to lead others. Act now. Start a new business.

Bible verse:

> *The* Lord *shall open unto thee his good treasure, the heaven to give the rain unto thy land in his season, and to bless all the work of thine hand: and thou shalt lend unto many nations, and thou shalt not borrow.*
>
> (DEUTERONOMY 28:12)

QUEEN OF CLUBS

Meaning: A dark-haired woman who's strong-willed, helpful, attractive. Nice, but inclined to be moody.

Action: Move yourself up front and center; accept the limelight.

Bible verse:

> *Arise, shine; for thy light is come, and the glory of the* Lord *is risen upon thee. For, behold, the darkness shall cover the earth, and gross darkness the people: but the* LORD *shall arise upon thee, and his glory shall be seen upon thee. And the Gentiles shall come to thy light, and kings to the brightness of thy rising.*
>
> (ISAIAH 60:1–3)

JACK OF CLUBS

Meaning: A reliable friend who has your back and will stand beside you; sincere but impatient.

Action: You are growing spiritually. Abundance and freedom are yours for the taking.

Bible verse:

> *One gives freely, yet grows all the richer; another withholds what he should give, and only suffers want. Whoever brings blessing will be enriched, and one who waters will himself be watered.*
>
> (PROVERBS 11:24–25)

TEN OF CLUBS

Meaning: You are overloaded, and your second sight has been blocked.

Action: A series of spiritual cleansings and road opening work is needed.

Bible verse:

> *Come, and let us return unto the* Lord*: for he hath torn, and he will heal us; he hath smitten, and he will bind us up. After two days will he revive us: in the third day he will raise us up, and we shall live in his sight. Then shall we know, if we follow on to know the* Lord*: his going forth is prepared as the morning; and he shall come unto us as the rain, as the latter and former rain unto the earth.*
>
> (HOSEA 6:1–3)

NINE OF CLUBS

Meaning: Feelings of confusion and being in a rut. Disputes with friends over money. Stubbornness.

Action: Stop, stand still, and focus on your goal. Do some spiritual cleansing.

Bible verse:

> *The Lord was pleased that Solomon had asked for this. So God said to him, "Since you have asked for this and not for long life or wealth for yourself, nor have asked for the death of your enemies but for discernment in administering justice, I will do what you have asked. I will give you a wise and discerning heart, so that there will never have been anyone like you, nor will there ever be."*
>
> (1 KINGS 3:10–12)

EIGHT OF CLUBS

Meaning: The time to act is now. All your wishes and desires are ready to become a reality. Stay focused.

Action: Don't yield to recklessness; think before you jump into something new, and watch out for your money.

Bible verse:

> *Know well the condition of your flocks, and give attention to your herds, for riches do not last forever; and does a crown endure to all generations?*
>
> (PROVERBS 27:23–24)

SEVEN OF CLUBS

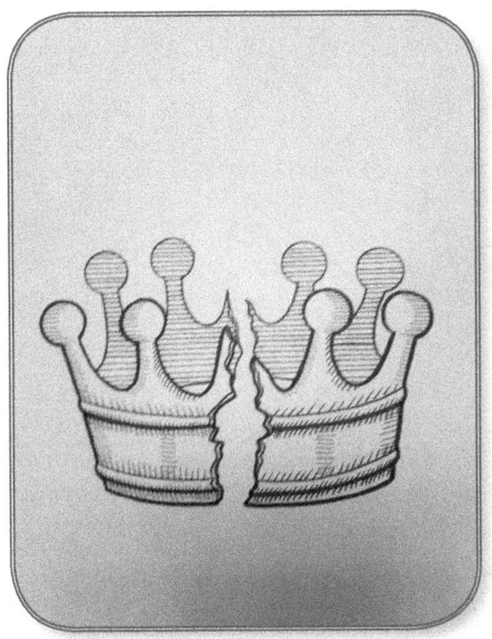

Meaning: You will be a success. You will be successful in removing all obstacles.

Action: You may have to defend yourself against an attack. It's time for defense and a strong wall of protection.

Bible verse:

> *Thy right hand, O Lord, is become glorious in power: thy right hand, O Lord, hath dashed in pieces the enemy. And in the greatness of thine excellency thou hast overthrown them that rose up against thee: thou sentest forth thy wrath, which consumed them as stubble.*
>
> (EXODUS 15:6–7)

SIX OF CLUBS

Meaning: Victory is yours. All problems are being moved out of the way. You have success.

Action: Now is the time to take that step forward and follow your dream.

Bible verse:

> *"One nation was being crushed by another and one city by another, because God was troubling them with every kind of distress. But as for you, be strong and do not give up, for your work will be rewarded."*
>
> (2 CHRONICLES 15:6–7)

FIVE OF CLUBS

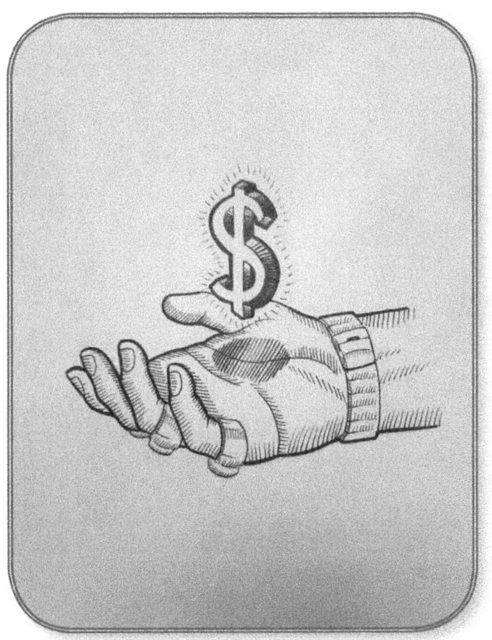

Meaning: You have conflicts that must be handled swiftly; don't stew over the situation. Take care of your business.

Action: Consider all of your possibilities before you act. Think before you leap.

Bible verse:

> *Now therefore, I pray thee, if I have found grace in thy sight, shew me now thy way, that I may know thee, that I may find grace in thy sight: and consider that this nation is thy people. And he said, My presence shall go with thee, and I will give thee rest.*
>
> (EXODUS 33:13–14)

FOUR OF CLUBS

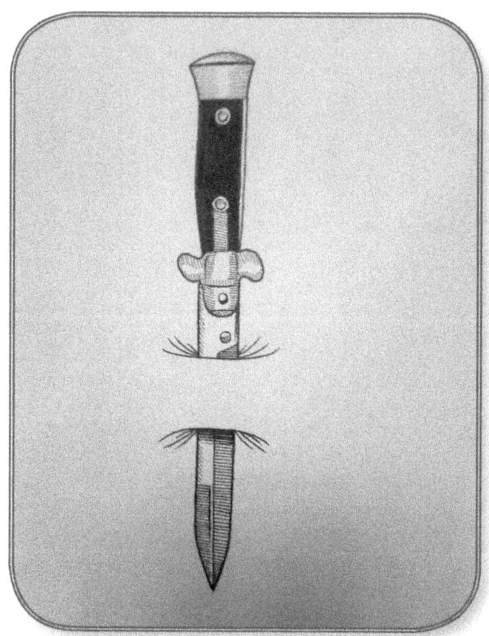

Meaning: You are building a strong foundation; take it to the crossroads for success.

Action: Watch your back. You are stable, strong, and ready to move forward. Stay focused and positive.

Bible verse:

> *And God blessed them. And God said to them, "Be fruitful and multiply and fill the earth and subdue it and have dominion over the fish of the sea and over the birds of the heavens and over every living thing that moves on the earth."*
>
> (GENESIS 1:28)

THREE OF CLUBS

Meaning: Interference from a friend could cost a relationship or cash; take the blinders off and see the real person.

Action: You are a total success and have achieved all your goals; it's time to move on to a new path.

Bible verse:

> *Happy art thou, O Israel: who is like unto thee, O people saved by the* Lord, *the shield of thy help, and who is the sword of thy excellency, And thine enemies shall be found liars unto thee; and thou shalt tread upon their high places.*
>
> (DEUTERONOMY 33:29)

TWO OF CLUBS

Meaning: Obstacles to success; malicious gossip, disappointment, and opposition.

Action: You are at a crossroads in your life. Choose wisely which bend you take; the wrong one can lead to disaster. It's time for some serious Conjure to remove the blocks and shut those mouths.

Bible verse:

> *And if ye go to war in your land against the enemy that oppresseth you, then ye shall blow an alarm with the trumpets; and ye shall be remembered before the* Lord *your God, and ye shall be saved from your enemies.*
>
> (NUMBERS 10:9)

SPADES

ACE OF SPADES

Meaning: Crossed conditions, roads closed, conflicts. A difficult love affair. Troubles await.

Action: Serious cleansing is needed here, followed by some protection Conjure. Follow through and you will make the right decisions.

Bible verse:

> *"Finally my brethren, be strong in the* L*ORD* *and in the power of his might. Put on the whole armor of God that ye may be able to stand against the wiles of the devil. For we wrestle not against flesh and blood, but against powers, against the rulers of the darkness of this world, against spiritual wickedness in high places. Wherefore take unto you the whole armor of God that ye may be able to withstand in the evil day, and have done all, to stand."*
>
> (EPHESIANS 6:10)

KING OF SPADES

Meaning: A successful man whose ambition overrides everything else; a self-centered man who is also self-serving.

Action: Make wise decisions, keep a clear head, and focus on balance. Don't be fooled.

Bible verse:

> *"The lofty looks of man shall be humbled, and the haughtiness of men shall be bowed down, and the* Lord *alone shall be exalted in that day. For the day of the* Lord *of hosts shall be upon every one that is proud and lofty, and upon every one that is lifted up; and he shall be brought low."*
>
> (ISAIAH 2:11–12)

QUEEN OF SPADES

Meaning: A dark-haired woman who is seductive, unscrupulous, fond of scandal, and open to bribery.

Action: Make good decisions. Act independently to avoid treachery, betrayal, and malice.

Bible verse:

> *"Let not thine heart decline to her ways, go not astray in her paths. For she cast down many wounded: yea, many strong men have been slain by her. Her house is the way to hell, going down to the chambers of death."*
>
> (PROVERBS 7:25–27)

JACK OF SPADES

Meaning: This person means well, but they are a hindrance in all work. Slow movement in projects. Blocks, cross condition, jealousy, very hostile environment or person.

Action: Perform a cut and clear.

Bible verse:

> *"If you listen carefully to what he says and do all that I say, I will be an enemy to your enemies and will oppose those who oppose you."*
>
> (EXODUS 23:22)

TEN OF SPADES

Meaning: A personal low with depression, worry, grief, and the imprisonment of one's spirit. Bad news, illness, an accident, bad luck, jinxed, or crossed.

Action: You are moving too fast; slow down. A strong cleansing is needed.

Bible verse:

> *A merry heart doeth good like a medicine: but a broken spirit drieth the bones.*
>
> (PROVERBS 17:22)

Or

> *"For I know the plans I have for you," declares the* Lord, *"plans to prosper you and not to harm you, plans to give you hope and a future."*
>
> (JEREMIAH 29:11)

NINE OF SPADES

Meaning: Bad luck, delays, quarrels, sleeplessness, sickness, losses, troubles, and family problems. Take action.

Action: Perform a strong spiritual cleansing and protection work.

Bible verse:

> *"But those who hope in the* Lord *will renew their strength. They will soar on wings like eagles; they will run and not grow weary, they will walk and not be faint."*
>
> (ISAIAH 40:31)

EIGHT OF SPADES

Meaning: Two-faced friends, disappointments, and opposition. A warning with regard to any business deals being worked on.

Action: Be cautious. You have been nailed down; a jinx or crossed condition needs to be removed.

Bible verse:

> *"No weapons formed against you shall prosper, and every tongue which rises against you in judgment you shall condemn. This is the heritage of the servants of the* LORD, *and their righteousness is from Me," says the* LORD.
>
> (ISAIAH 54:7)

SEVEN OF SPADES

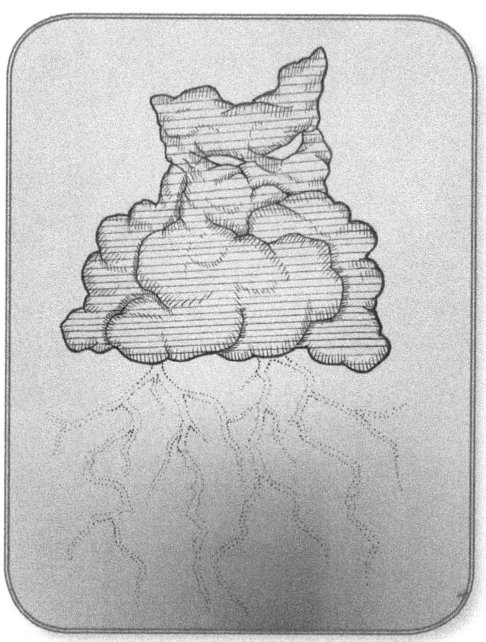

Meaning: Beware of being deceived by someone you trust. Quarrels. Stress from overdue bills.

Action: You are on overload. Do a set of five cleansing baths to cut and clear the battles and gain peace of mind.

Bible verse:

> *"And the LORD will take away from you all sickness, and will afflict you with none of the terrible diseases of Egypt which you have known, but will lay them on all those who hate you."*
>
> (DEUTERONOMY 7:15)

SIX OF SPADES

Meaning: Help is on its way; you will soon solve the problems you are facing.

Action: The storms have lifted. Love, prosperity, and happiness are yours for the taking.

Bible verse:

> *Blessed is the man that trusteth in the* Lord, *and whose hope the* Lord *is.*
>
> *For he shall be as a tree planted by the waters, and that spreadeth out her roots by the river, and shall not see when heat cometh, but her leaf shall be green; and shall not be careful in the year of drought, neither shall cease from yielding fruit.*
>
> (JEREMIAH 17:7–8)

FIVE OF SPADES

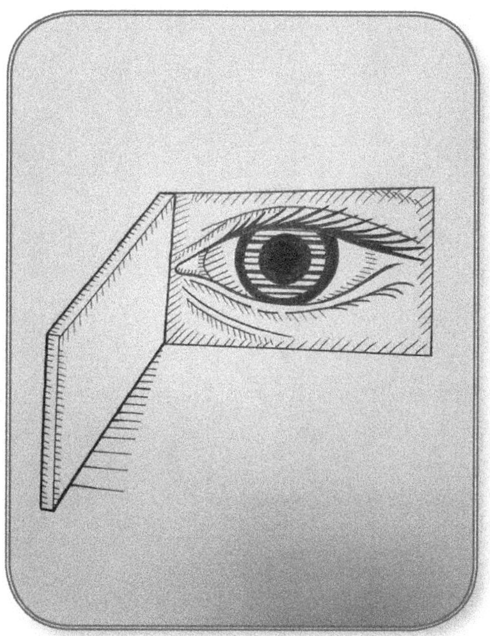

Meaning: Stop trying to prove you know what is best; this causes anxiety and setbacks.

Action: Control your temper. Be flexible. Listen and look at the whole picture; the answer is right in front of you.

Bible verse:

> *Trust in the LORD with all thine heart; and lean not unto thine own understanding. In all thy ways acknowledge him, and he shall direct thy paths.*
>
> (PROVERBS 3:5–6)

FOUR OF SPADES

Meaning: Jealousy, business troubles, sickness, minor misfortunes, or delays in a project.

Action: Stop! Be still and take time to focus and relax. You can fix the problem.

Bible verse:

> *The Spirit of the* Lord *God is upon me, because the* Lord *hath anointed me to bring good news to the poor; he has sent me to bind up the brokenhearted, to proclaim liberty to the captives, and the opening of the prison to those who are bound;*
>
> *To proclaim the year of the* Lord*'s favor, and the day of vengeance of our God; to comfort all who mourn;*

To grant to those who mourn in Zion—to give them a beautiful headdress instead of ashes, the oil of gladness instead of mourning, the garment of praise instead of a faint spirit; that they may be called oaks of righteousness, the planting of the Lord, that he may be glorified.

(ISAIAH 61:1–3)

THREE OF SPADES

Meaning: Problems in a relationship, especially a cheating partner; inconstancy in the people around you.

Action: Now that you're aware of the problem, you can fix it.

Bible verse:

> *Whoever walks in integrity walks securely, but he who makes his ways crooked will be found out.*
>
> (PROVERBS 10:9)

TWO OF SPADES

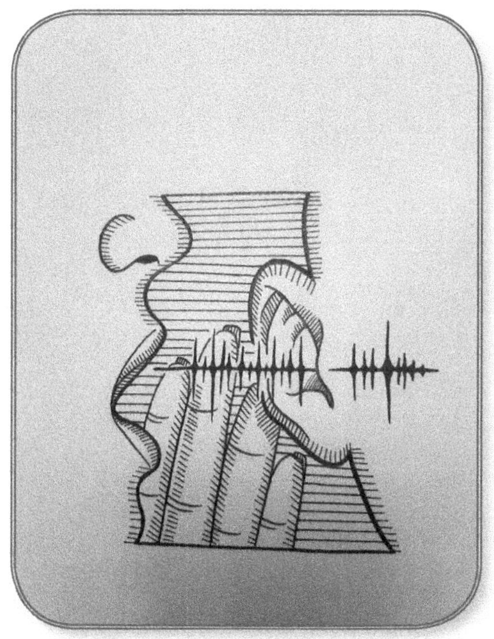

Meaning: A scandal. Someone is talking about you. Danger of deceit, change for the worse in a situation.

Action: Perform a cleansing and protection work.

Bible verse:

> *"I will make you a wall to this people,*
> *a fortified wall of bronze;*
> *they will fight against you*
> *but will not overcome you,*
> *for I am with you*
> *to rescue and save you,*
> *declares the* Lord.
> *I will save you from the hands of the wicked*
> *and deliver you from the grasp of the cruel."*
>
> (JEREMIAH 15:20–21)

JOKERS

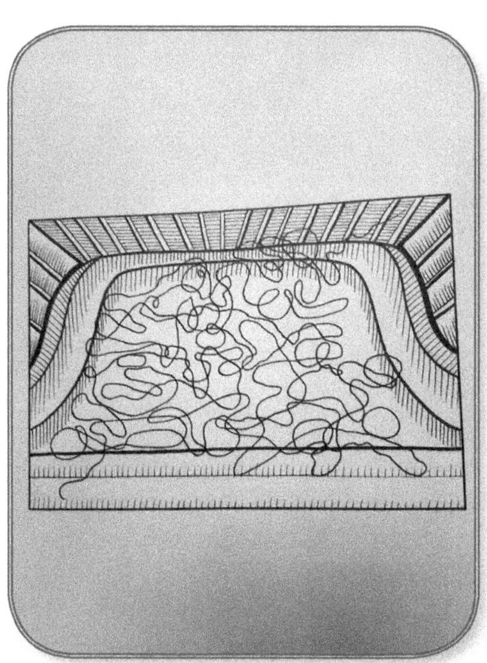

I was taught that the jokers in the deck represent the ancestors and the spirits that walk with us. Some Christians will say it is against God's will that we remember and honor our ancestors. Yet, in many places in the Bible it speaks of this. If you look at Deuteronomy, you will see that the ancestors are not forgotten. Most of the time, when the Bible is speaking of the ancestors they will call them your "fathers."

> *That he may establish thee to day for a people unto himself, and that he may be unto thee a God, as he hath said unto thee, and as he hath sworn unto thy fathers, to Abraham, to Isaac, and to Jacob.*
>
> (DEUTERONOMY 29:13)

As you can see in Deuteronomy 29:13, it is nothing new that folks name their ancestors when they are honoring them. Folks need to learn the difference between honoring and worshiping. Here are a few more verses about the ancestors:

> *But your dead will live, Lord;*
> *their bodies will rise—*
> *let those who dwell in the dust*
> *wake up and shout for joy—*
> *your dew is like the dew of the morning;*
> *the earth will give birth to her dead.*
>
> (ISAIAH 26:19)

> *But this happened that we might not rely on ourselves but on God, who raises the dead. He has delivered us from such a deadly peril, and he will deliver us again. On him we have set our hope that he will continue to deliver us, as you help us by your prayers. Then many will give thanks on our behalf for the gracious favor granted us in answer to the prayers of many."*
>
> (2 CORINTHIANS 1:9–11)

LAYOUTS

I work with a few different card layouts. I know folks have their own ways of laying out their cards. The layouts that I share here are ones I have used for years.

A general note to start: the one thing that you should always remember is that nothing is written in stone; any card reading can be changed if you change the situation. I had a client who went to a woman for a reading, and by the time she got out of there she was so scared she drove straight over to see me. That reader had her terrified! I think she was trying to get the client to commit to some type of work or something.

The thing is, you should never, ever, *ever* tell somebody that a reading cannot be changed—because that is absolutely not true. If you see an issue or you see something could possibly be going wrong, then tell them of it in a calm way, not in dire straits. If possible, tell them some things they can do for themselves to help change the outcome. Always put your client first.

Second, I'm not sure why, but some folks want to have a reading but don't want to admit that the cards are right. I have had clients deny a situation until the last minute when I tell them I am stopping the reading and refunding their money because I can't help them if they don't want to help themselves. They are never expecting that, so they usually break down and spill the truth. Nine times out of ten the cards are spot-on. I'm just not going to mess around and waste my time when there are other folks who need my help!

For example, say I'm doing a layout for a woman who would like to know what her love life holds for her. I shuffle the cards and lay out the ace of diamonds, which represents money, the ten of hearts, which represents love and marriage, and the seven of spades, which is the kicker. As an experienced reader, these cards are telling me that money is a big decision in this marriage proposal, and the seven of spades in particular tells me that my client is compelled to marry because of the money. At this point I lay out three more cards to see what else is going on. Then I tell the client what I see.

When I read the cards, I will show the client which card is saying what. So in this layout I would say something like, "The ace of diamonds is very good for the foundation of the reading; it represents prosperity—and a lots of it."

Then I would lay down the next card, the ten of diamonds, and I would say, "We've got the ten of diamonds. I see that this is going to be a very prosperous marriage."

When I lay down the seven of spades, I would say something like, "Oh, I see that this is a marriage of convenience. The marriage is mostly about money even though there are feelings involved."

As a good reader, simply say that you are only sharing what the cards are showing. Then it's up to the client to say, "Yes, it's true," or "No, you're way off base." Then you can say, "Do you have another question? Is there anything else that I can help you with?" Be as polite as possible. It is not your place to try to convince a client that what the cards are saying is the truth. It is simply your job to lay the cards out and convey the story that the cards tell.

In this line of work, I run into all types of people. Some want the truth and admit to it, and others deny everything that the cards are trying to tell them. But it's not my place to shove it in their faces. It is my place to simply read the cards, help if I can, be polite if I can't, and send them on their way.

I'm bringing this up because there could be young readers reading this, and I have seen old, seasoned readers get upset when the folks they are reading for disagree with them. I have seen some be so rude, it embarrassed me the way they talked to the person sitting at their table. If you are going to perform readings for others, you cannot take it personally when folks disagree with you. It's best to just be as kind and polite as possible.

It may seem like a lot of work or a lot to learn in order to read the cards, but it's really not—because the more you work with your cards and your ancestors, the stronger your intuition will become and the easier it will be for you to understand what the ancestors are trying to convey. I've been reading cards since I was sixteen, and I still have to study the cards and listen closely. Once you are in a reading mode, it's no longer about you and what you think the cards mean; it's about you listening to what spirit is telling you. Take your time. It will be easier than you think if you have a strong connection with your ancestors, because they truly speak to you through the cards. Just relax and don't overthink it.

Now on to the layouts!

CROSS

The cross layout is very important to me, and it is one of my favorite layouts because Mr. Robert taught me. Mr. Robert was my mentor, may he rise in power. He taught me everything I know about Father Blackhawk, who was a Sauk medicine man and war chief. Blackhawk is one of the spirits I honor.

It took me a while to get this layout even though it seems so simple. I sat at the table with him for what seemed like hours going over it. Trust and believe, I will never forget it. Use this layout when you want to find out the foundation of an issue.

The first card you lay down is the foundation. That is the reason for the reading. Then you lay a card at the top. Then you lay a card at the bottom. Then you lay a card to the right and a card to the left. You then pull one more card.

You may be thinking, *Wow that seems like a pretty simple layout. What was the issue?* Well, the issue was that I laid the cards out with the foundation card first, then the top one, then the bottom one, and then I went from *left to right*. I tell you, Mr. Robert made me redo that layout I don't know how many times, until he busted out laughing because I truly didn't understand what I was doing.

"Why are you crossing yourself?" He asked. I guess he finally felt sorry for me.

"What you talking about, Mr. Robert? I'm not crossing myself," I replied.

"Really, you're not?"

"No, sir." Now I was getting aggravated.

"Okay, if you are not crossing yourself, then shuffle the cards and lay them down again just like you've been laying them down."

I shuffled the cards and put the foundation card down. *That was one.* Then a card on top. *Two.* Then a card on the bottom. *Three.* Then a card on the left. *Four.* And one to the right. *Five.* Then it dawned on me what I'd been doing, and the expression on my face cracked him up that much more. I thought he was going to fall out of the chair! And then I started laughing. He was right. I *was* crossing up the foundation of the reading by crossing over it from left to right.

Anytime you do any type of setup in Conjure work and you go from left to right, you are nailing that setup down, be it good or bad. That means that if it was a horrible card, it was nailed into place. This is a lesson I will never forget, and every time I lay the cards out I think of Mr. Robert and I think of that day. So remember: anytime you are laying the cards out in any kind of setup, do not cross from left to right.

To do this layout, start by shuffling your cards and then lay down the first card. This is the foundation. That is the heart or reason for the reading.

Then you lay a card at the top, which is what is covering you; it also represents what is going on at this moment.

The third card, below the foundation card, is what is walking with you—what exactly is going on at the time of the reading. Usually by the time I get just those three cards laid out in a column I have a good insight about what is truly going on.

The next card that is laid out goes to the right—that could be the past or something that is happening now; it just depends on the card and the other cards that are laid out.

Then you have the card that goes to the left. This card represents what could happen. It goes along with the last card, which covers the foundation card. Those two cards usually work together to give you an outcome of the situation if things are not changed up. So, to review:

- Card one is the foundation
- Card two is what is covering you
- Card three is what is walking with you
- Card four is what is behind you
- Card five is what is in front of you
- Card six is the outcome if nothing is changed

HOLY TRINITY CROSSROADS

This unique spread is powerful because you are combining two works: the power of the Holy Trinity, as shown by the pyramid; and the crossroads, because the base of the spread is four cards, which is where you'll find the answer. (Note that the crossroads does not mean a literal cross; the crossroads is represented by the number four, and there are four cards at the bottom of the layout.) This spread is used when you need to find out something specific. If you are on the lookout, then this spread will lead you to the truth.

To do the layout, begin by shuffling the playing cards while petitioning God and your ancestors to open your eyes and find you the truth. Starting at the top, lay one card out. Then lay two cards below the first, followed by three cards, then four. You should have a pyramid with four rows, like this:

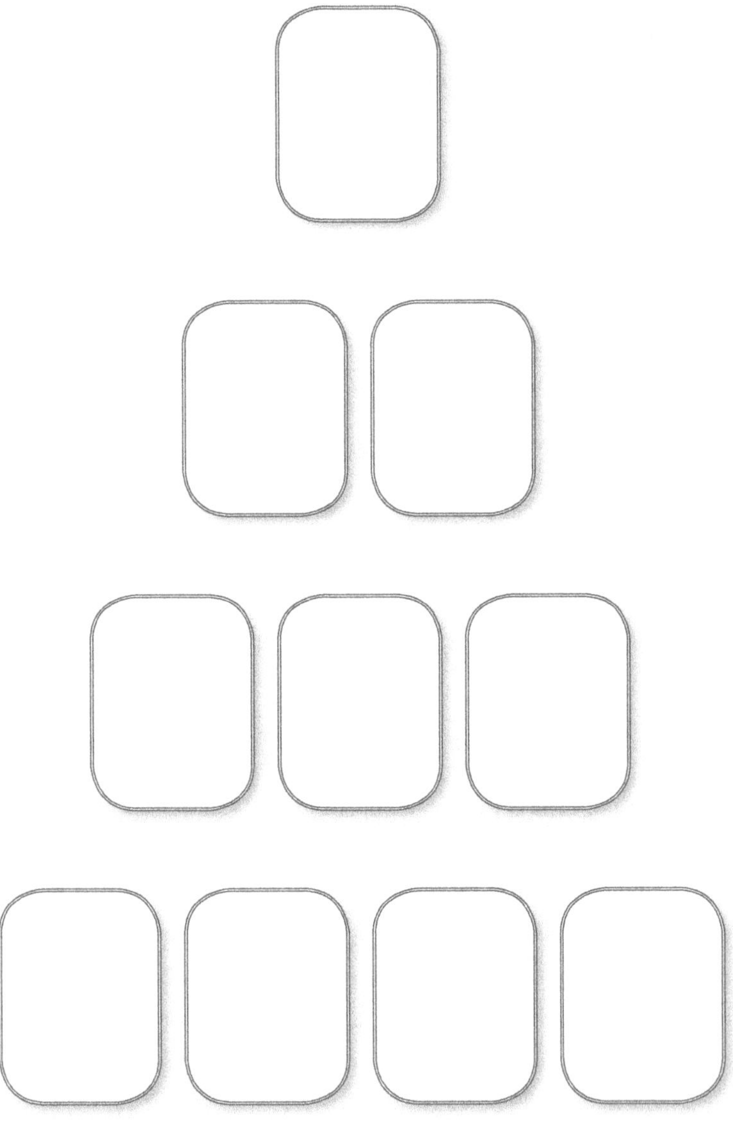

To read the layout, start with the top card and go from there.

- Row 1 (top row): What is going on at this moment with the petitioner and what the outcome could be.
- Rows 2 and 3: What can be done to change the situation and what can be foretold. For example, if the petitioner card is negative or shows any blocks, look to the second and third rows to see how long the blocks will last.
- Row 4: The solution to the petitioner's problem.

In this layout everything is tied together, and your job as a reader is to put all the pieces together. Remember that each card has its own meaning in a layout, but that meaning can be twisted around by the other cards around it. Be mindful of this. You can't base your whole reading on one or two cards; you have to look at the whole picture and see how all the cards interact with each other to get the full story.

All the cards in this spread are important, but the cards you need to really pay attention to are the top card and the bottom cards, since the top card shows you what it is you will face and the bottom cards tell you what the situation is and what the outcome could be. The strongest cards in the whole reading are the base cards because they are set in the shape of a cross. We all know there is power in the sign of a cross. Spirit sits in the center of the cross.

If you look at the pyramid, you will see that the pyramid shows your power starting with the first card and how to build up your power with the other cards. The base cards tell you how successful you will be or if there are any blocks or crossed conditions going on. You really need to pay attention so you can fix any issues that might show up in the layout.

This layout works with the power of the Holy Trinity and the power of the cross! That makes this layout very powerful.

You can also incorporate this spread into work with your ancestors. For example, if you want to draw success and the cards show you what to do, then burn a candle or Conjure lamp on your spread every day while praying your petition and prayers to the ancestors.

If your layout is full of cards that represent blocks or crossed conditions and the cards around them don't show anything being lifted, then take this as a sign that you need to do some cleansing or reversal work. I've added a Holy Trinity Reversal layout next to reverse any condition that may be there.

HOLY TRINITY REVERSAL

If you are feeling stuck or confused, or have discovered through divination that your roads are blocked, this spread is what you need to remove those blocks and open your roads.

This layout works just like the Holy Trinity Crossroads layout—except this time you will be laying the cards out in reverse. The layout will help you see where the blocks are, and how they are affecting your life. It will also show if your work will be a success or not. If the cards don't have a positive layout, then you can lay a fifth row on top of the first one and see if the situation will be changed.

For this layout, start the pyramid with four cards in the first row and remove a card from each row until the last and final row has only one.

The first row lays out the problem, or shows the block. Each of the four cards reveals the work you need to do to remove or reverse the block.

The second row shows how uncrossing work will affect the situation. The cards in that row will tell you how it all plays out in your favor or against you.

The third row tells you what will happen, what will take place to get the job done.

The final card, which is your spirit, tells how successful your work will be. It is important that the final card comes out cleansed and uncrossed. You don't want your spirit all crossed up and in a jam.

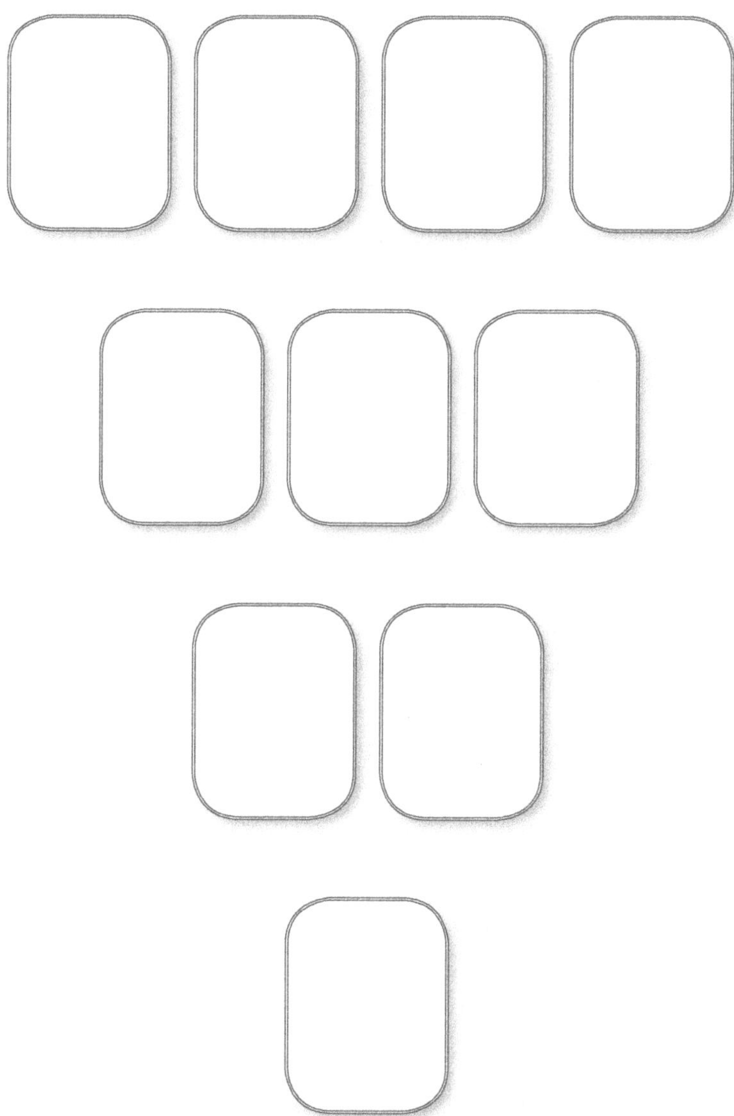

The pyramid reversal spread is strong because you start off at four cards and take one away until it ends up with one card: your spirit. As you read the cards, you're removing the block. The idea is that you are knocking anything down that is in your way—you are taking power away from the block and placing it back where it belongs. Since you are dealing with spirit, you need to petition your ancestors to destroy the blocks that are binding and blocking you.

ALTERNATIVE REVERSAL WORKING

This next working is simply a different way to achieve the same goal reversal. It's a simple but strong work.

First, lay out a white prayer cloth on which you have prayed the Holy Spirit onto your working table. Place a photo of yourself in the center of the prayer cloth and petition God for help.

Sprinkle some dirt from three holy places on the prayer cloth, starting at the photo in the center and going outward toward the edges. Make sure your photo is covered with dirt. Petition God and your ancestors to protect you and remove any blocks that bind and cross you. If you notice, you are going counterclockwise, which will undo any blocks or crossed conditions that may be trying to hold you down.

Take out your cards and shuffle them well. Then call on the Holy Trinity and your ancestors. Petition them to give you the insight you need to fix the issues at hand. Petition your ancestors to fight for you and to show you what you need to do in order to remove the crossed condition. Petition them to show you in a way you will understand. Lay the cards on top of the dirt in the reversal pyramid. Read the cards, paying close attention to what your ancestors are telling you.

After reading the cards, cleanse yourself with a white candle. Starting at the crown of your head and going downward to the bottom of your feet, push whatever is there away from you and into the ground. (You could also use a black candle instead of a white one—it all depends on your ancestors.) Keep going over your body until you feel a shift in the candle. It may become warm, or feel heavier or lighter—it all depends on your ancestors and spirits as to how they remove the condition. Once you are done with the rub down, light the candle on your prayer cloth and petition God and your ancestors to set you free from the binds that are trying to hold you down.

If you have really strong blocks on you, get a piece of chain and cleanse yourself with it, starting at the crown of your head and going downward just like you did the candle. If you want to reverse the condition, you can also go around your head and body counterclockwise until you feel a release. Then break the chain! Remove half of the chain from the altar and wrap the other half around the candle for the ancestors to work with, so they can reverse the condition and bind your enemies with it.

COMBINATIONS

There is more to reading the cards than just understanding their meanings and placing them in a certain layout. You also need to get a feel for the relationships between the cards. Reading the cards is like putting together a puzzle. I have found that when certain cards fall together, there are usually certain things going on in the person's life. The cards will always tell the full story.

This is the main reason why your divination tools should be given to your ancestors to speak through. Because even though a card means a certain thing, you may get a different type of message from your ancestors and your spirits. Always go with their message. The best way to interpret the cards is to listen to that little inner voice that guides you.

The most important thing about this work is to be able to discern the difference between what we are thinking and what spirit is sharing with us. It has taken me many years of working with my ancestors to get an open line of communication between them and me. Your ancestors should be your first go-to when you need help.

COMMON COMBINATIONS

Here you will find a few combinations and how I see them. There are many more—this is just a small selection to give you an idea. You may find that the combinations feel different to you; that you don't see the combinations the way I have them written. That's fine. Because we all have different spirits, and different ancestors that walk with us, no two people will ever discern anything the same. You have to learn to interpret your readings by listening to what your ancestors and the spirits share with you.

- Ace of diamonds + ten of hearts: The couple could be headed for marriage.
- Ace of diamonds + ten of diamonds: This marriage is for money only. If the seven of spades falls nearby, then the person is being compelled into the marriage.
- Ace of diamonds + six of spades: Something is going to cost you money, or you won't get the raise you are looking for.
- Ace of diamonds + seven of hearts: You have a rival. If the ace of hearts falls nearby, then someone is after your lover.
- Ace of clubs among diamonds: Total success.
- King, queen, or jack between two cards of same number: Someone will offer you their support in a serious situation.
- King or queen between two jacks: You need protection from your enemies.
- Queen of spades between a king + a queen: A warning of a possible breakup.
- Jack next to king or queen: You need protection work done.
- Jack of spades among several diamonds: There's an argument about money.
- Seven, ten, and three of Diamonds: A secret will be told.
- Seven + eight of diamonds: Keep your business in your own house or it will be told. Gossip about you is running wild.

- Eight + nine of spades or nine + ten of spades: A warning of health problems.
- Ten of diamonds + ten of clubs: You have the Midas touch.
- Ten of hearts + king and queen of hearts: A possible wedding.
- Ten of diamonds + seven of spades: Roadblocks and delays are blocking your success. Do a cleansing.
- Five + eight of spades: A jealous rival is stalking you. Be very careful. It's time for a cut and clear.
- Four of diamonds + four of spades: You are being crossed and forced to make a decision against your will.

Like the combination of cards, if you get different suits but the same multiples of cards, it can change the whole reading. If you get two of the same card, then it is a strong possibility that those cards are going to change the reading up.

Here's an example: Let's say I have a client who is thinking about going into business with a partner. The client contacts me and asks me to do a reading on this to make sure they are not making a mistake. I lay out the cards and get the ace of spades and the ace of diamonds. This tells me that even though the business may be prosperous, it is going to be very difficult. The ace of spades and the ace of diamonds together represent a difficult partnership. That in itself would be a red flag, although I'm the type of worker who believes that anything could change and any reading can be changed.

I lay down two more cards: the five of diamonds and the five of spades. So for me, five represents the crossroads—that's the four corners, and spirit in the middle. The way I was taught to read, multiple fives in a layout represents disappointment, change, and closed roads. And getting two fives after laying down the ace of spades and the ace of diamonds is red flags everywhere, as far as I'm concerned.

So, I would say to my client that if they are going to do this partnership, they should probably do some heavy cleansing and road opening work before they sign any paperwork or make any other formal commitments. It is my responsibility as a professional reader to give my client the best advice I can per the reading—not my feelings, not what I think they should do. It's my responsibility to simply tell them what I see and give them the option of fixing it or not.

When you are doing a reading, keep in mind that none of the cards stand alone in a reading. It is the combination of all the cards laid down that tell the story of what spirit is trying to convey to you. Just be mindful when you're doing readings, because you do hold other folks' lives in your hands. There are some folks who won't make a move without a reading, so just keep that in mind.

MULTIPLES

Following are some more combinations of cards. If they fall in multiples of two, three, or four in a reading, there's a stronger possibility the fortune will be true.

- Ace—new beginnings, reuniting, good news, lucky breaks
- Spades and diamonds: difficult marriage or partnership
- Two—opposition, separation, reaching a crossroads
- Three—roads are opened, a line of communication is opened, success
- Four—a shaky foundation, crossed condition, witchcraft
- Five—change, roads are closed, disappointments
- Six—contradictions, hard work, blocks
- Seven—gossip, brief illnesses, someone is trying to set you up

- Eight—indiscretion, crossed condition, blocks
- Nine—prosperity, good health, roads are opened
- Ten—completion, circumstances improve, total success
- Jack—youth, disagreements, false friends, quarrels, battles
- Queen—mature female
- *Two queens:* two-faced female friend, gossip, betrayal of confidence, scandals
- King—mature male, business partnership, support, success, timing

TIMING

Each suit represents a certain time of year. The suit that shows up the most in a reading will give you an idea about when the event could happen.

- Diamonds—spring
- Hearts—summer
- Clubs—autumn
- Spades—winter

MONTHS

Just as the suits represent the time of year, they can also represent the months of the year. Following is a list to help you determine when an event may happen.

- Jack of clubs—January, February, March
- Jack of hearts—April, May, June
- Jack of diamonds—July, August, September
- Jack of spades—October, November, December

LISTEN TO THEM THREES

The cards have many different meanings when they fall in a reading, and there is more than one of the same card even though it might be a different suit. If you have three aces in a layout, this could represent a new birth in the family, a new job, a new love, or a new home. When there are three or more of the same card in a reading, this changes the whole meaning of the story. This is where your discernment is needed, and you need to have a strong connection with your ancestors and the spirits that walk with you in order to be able to give the right information to the client.

- Three aces means there will be a birth, a fresh start, a new love, or a new job
- Three twos means things could be changing for better or for worse, depending on the surrounding cards
- Three threes means the moves you need to make become clear and you know if it is the thing to do or not by the surrounding cards
- Three fours means you have a strong foundation and you should keep moving forward
- Three fives means you will run into a snag in your plans because there are hidden issues that you are not aware of
- Three sixes means changes for the better are coming; blocks are being moved out of the way
- Three sevens means now is the time to plant the seeds for the new ideas you have; it's time to move forward
- Three eights means you may be dealing with cranky folks and some friendships may be put to the test
- Three nines means it's time to get off the stick and move forward; you are wasting time

- Three tens means your goal is at hand; it's time to finish what you started
- Three jacks means you are taking too many chances; slow down and think before you move forward
- Three queens means you have the power and the knowledge to make the needed changes
- Three kings means you are on the right track; keep moving forward in the direction you are headed

WORKINGS

I learned a long time ago how to work with the cards doing root work. I believe that each of the cards holds the spirit and that when you combine that card with Conjure work you can't go wrong. These are easy but powerful works that I do myself quite often for clients, family members, and myself when I need it.

You don't need a lot to do these works; you just need a deck of cards, some candles, a Bible, maybe a few roots and herbs, and your ancestor altar (unless the work is being done with Saint Martha). There is no work that can't be done working with the cards. The cards represent the petition for the work, plus you are getting the extra power that the card holds. I want to share a few different types of work, such as work for success, for money, for love, for a peaceful home, and for justice. With these works you should have an idea of how to pick your own combination of cards and how to pick your own prayers and Bible verses—this is just a foundation for you to grow from.

I would like to place a little note of caution here: remember that every action causes a reaction, and you and you alone are responsible for the works that you do. If you do unjustified works against someone and your target has enough spiritual knowledge to do reversal or uncrossing work, you will be hit with your own work. Some folks believe that Conjure work has no rules or anything that folks have to abide by. This is not true. What is true is that you can do any work that is justified. That doesn't mean that just because somebody makes you mad, you can start throwing at them and that's justified.

You should always do a divination first to check and see if you even have the right to do the work that you are trying to do. Be mindful that no one is responsible for your actions but you. There is no fairy godmother that's going to take the blame for the things you do if you do unjustified works; even your ancestors probably would not protect you. As the old saying goes, don't throw if you don't want to get thrown at!

Always use your wisdom and your knowledge with responsibility, and know that when you start a work and you give it to your ancestors or another spirit, that work is out of your hands. There's no calling it back or saying "I'm sorry." There are absolutely no takebacks, so just be mindful of your actions because they really are your responsibility.

SUCCESS WORK

Who doesn't want to draw a little more success into their life? The first work I would like to share with you is for success in whatever endeavor you may be trying to make fruitful.

Work for Success

You will need:

- Ace of clubs
- Eight of diamonds
- Ten of diamonds
- A cool glass of water
- 1 white candle
- A Bible
- 1 yellow candle
- 1 blue candle
- 1 green candle

Spread a white handkerchief on your altar. Place the glass of water and the white candle on your altar and open your Bible to Genesis 30:43. Once you get everything set up, light the candle and call on your ancestors to uplift you to success.

Lay down the ace of clubs first. This is your foundation card. It means it's time to move into action; harmony, achievements, love, peace of mind, professional success.

Lay down the eight of diamonds to the right to the right of that. It means hard work brings success and money, so you will have success.

The last card, laid on the left, is the ten of diamonds, which means total success, money, love, joy.

Then set the yellow candle on top of the foundation card, the blue candle on top of the eight of diamonds, and the green candle on top of the ten of diamonds. (You may feel like you need to work with different colored candles than the ones I used, and that's all good and fine. There is no right way or wrong way to do this; follow where your spirit leads you.)

When you have everything in place, pick up the yellow candle and call on your ancestors and then say your prayers and petition into the candle. Set it back on your card and light it. Pick up the blue candle to the right and repeat the same process, then pick up the green candle to the left and say your prayers and petitions into it, set it down, and light it. Once all the candles are lit, pray Genesis 30:43 over the setup three times:

> *In this way the man grew exceedingly prosperous and*
> *came to own large flocks, and female and male servants,*
> *and camels and donkeys.*
>
> (GENESIS 30:43)

It's a good idea to just sit there and contemplate on the work at hand.

When I do this type of work, I leave my candles burning. But if you are afraid to leave your candles burning, you can snuff them out and restart the work the next day when the hands of the clock are moving upward. I do this sometimes when I'm trying to give the work a rest for a few hours, and sometimes it actually helps the work.

Keep this going until you have the success you are looking for. As always, repeat as needed.

MONEY WORK

In this day and time, there never seems to be enough money to go around. It seems like in today's world money goes as fast as you make it. There are times when things come up that are expensive, and I don't feel like it's being greedy to do a money work to draw in the extra prosperity that is needed. I will never believe that God or your higher power or whatever you want to call it means for us to be broke down and scratching for everything that we get. I also don't believe that the ancestors want us to be struggling. So I personally don't see anything wrong with doing prosperity work or Crown of Success work to help keep the money flowing.

When I wrote *Hoodoo Money Conjure* years ago, someone got on to me about putting out works for prosperity and drawing money. They felt like it wasn't safe to be doing money work, because in order to get money something bad had to happen. And I don't disagree with that; but I *do* disagree with the way they were saying it. I feel that we should have everything that we need and everything that we want if we are willing to work for it. For me, doing money work, or doing work to pay a bill, or doing work to help the client get a job and make money, is no different than going to church and praying for success and prosperity. It's the same thing; it's all in your mind-set.

My mama, God rest her soul, had a funny way of looking at money. But I guess it's from the way she was raised. Growing up, she figured that if you had clothes to wear, a place to live, and food to eat, then you were rich and you had enough. It took me a long time to get myself out of that way of thinking, and that's when I wrote *Hoodoo Money Conjure*. Because I thought if others think that way too, things need to change.

I will never believe that my ancestors want me to be living hand to mouth, the way they had to live. They already went through all that struggle, and I don't feel like they want me to go through it. I truly feel that it would be an insult to them for me not to work and try to be all I can be and try to keep building the foundation for the next generation.

I will always work toward prosperity for my family so that the next generation will have a foundation to grow. With that being said, I want to say this also: you can do all the money Conjure in the world, but if you don't do your part, it's not going to last. You cannot do prosperity work and then not follow through and still have the work be effective. Everything costs something; there is absolutely nothing free in this life. Somebody somewhere is going to have to pay for it. So I don't want you to think that you can just do money work and money will start falling out of the sky. Life ain't like that. You are going to have to do your part.

Work for Money

You need to do at least three cleansing baths before you start. On the fourth day, you can do the work.

You will need:

- A few teaspoons of dirt from your front door and the four corners of your home
- A photo of yourself
- 1 white candle
- 2 blue candles
- 2 green candles
- Six of clubs

- Four of clubs
- Ace of clubs
- Ten of diamonds

First, gather the dirt from the front door of your home and the four corners of the house, and select a photo of yourself. Once you have your dirt and your photo, set up a small altar with those two pieces in the center. Cover the photo with the dirt, and then place your white candle on top.

Then place the six of clubs at the top, which means victory is yours, all problems are being moved out of the way, and you have success.

Place the four of clubs at the bottom, which means you are building a strong foundation; take it to the crossroads for success.

Place the ten of diamonds to the right, which means total success, money, love, and joy.

And finally, place the ace of clubs to the left. This means it's time to move into action. Harmony, achievements, love, peace of mind, professional success.

Set one blue candle on the top of the six of clubs, one green candle on the ten of diamonds, one blue candle on the four of clubs, and one green candle on the ace of clubs.

Call on your ancestors and say your prayer and petitions over your altar. Light the white candle first, then move on to the other candles, picking each one up and praying Isaiah 32:17–18 into the candle before lighting it:

> *The fruit of righteousness will be peace; the effect of righteousness will be quietness and confidence forever. My people will live in peaceful dwelling places, in secure homes, in undisturbed places of rest.*

Repeat the process until all the candles are lit. Go back to your altar at least three times a day and pray Isaiah 32:17–18 over your setup.

There is a little trick that you can do to help this work along. I was taught that you should always do more than one thing in order to make your work a success, so every day take a little bit of change out of your wallet and place it around the white candle. As you do this, say, "I received money today." Do this every single day.

Don't worry about the where the money is coming from. Don't focus on any of that. Simply trust that your ancestors and the spirits that walk with you will provide for you. All you have to do is do the work, do your part. Don't think you can sit at home watching TV all day eating bonbons and money's going to come blowing in. You have to work in order to have prosperity.

LOVE WORK

I wasn't sure that I was going to even put in a work dealing with love. I decided to add one, though, because there are so many folks out there searching for love and they can't seem to find true love or the right partner. I learned a very long time ago that if you are going to search for a partner or spouse the best way is to do spiritual cleansing on yourself first. And you may say, *Oh my Lord, I do cleansings all the time. I'm spiritually cleansed,* and that may be true; but if you have had serious relationship problems in the past, and you always seem to pick the wrong type of person to get into a relationship with, you might just need to do some spiritual cleansing and healing on yourself before you try to get into another relationship. I'm not here to preach or to tell anybody what to do, but I figure if you're reading this then you must need the information on how to do the work, or you may just want to start fresh—and that's fine. I want to explain myself when I say that if you are trying to do love work that you should do a cleansing first. This is why we draw what our spirit holds. Let me repeat that one more time: we draw what our spirit holds.

If you have been hurt in past relationships or your heart has been broken or you cannot trust your partner, then you need to do some cleansing work and some good soul-searching before you try to draw someone else into your life. If you don't, then you are going to draw those same problems every time because that is what you are carrying in your spirit. That is what you are telling the spirits that walk with you, your ancestors, and the universe: that you believe the things that you think about yourself and any partner you may get. The old saying "We are what we think" is literally true. If you think you're unlovable, you'll never find a partner that you can trust, everyone is going to abuse you and use you in a relationship, then that is exactly what you are going to get. Even if you say your life is great and everything is beautiful and the sun is shining and the birds are singing.

For this next work, you need the dirt from the corners of your house and the front and back doors—because that is where you live and that is where you are trying to draw love to. That is where you will want your partner to be. You'll also need lavender because it soothes the spirit and takes tension away; rose petals because rose is seen as the flower of love; lovage because it not only draws love but also promotes self-love; and orange peel because it's known for its attraction properties. The combination of all these ingredients is very strong to not only draw, but also promote, love, which is what this work is all about.

Also, let me explain the color choices for the candles you'll use. I like to explain the works because I don't expect anybody to follow me blindly and just do something because I wrote about it; I like for folks to know why they are working with this or working with that. I like to work with purple because it promotes self-power. I think the red candles explain themselves; not only do they promote love, but they also represent the blood. I figure the black candle might be the one that makes some folks nervous. I could have picked up a white candle instead, but I didn't, because black absorbs. We need the black candle to absorb and burn away past defeats. I know some folks fear black candles. I work with them a lot for cleansings and reversals in uncrossings because the black truly absorbs the conditions that are there. Here's a thought: Have you ever worn a black shirt on a hot summer day? If so, then you know how hot that shirt got, because it drew the sun and that heat to it. So then why wouldn't it pull off a crossed condition, blocks, or anything else that is on you?

For this work, we will petition Saint Martha. I have worked with Saint Martha for more years than I can remember—longer than I've lived in this house, and I've lived here for over thirty years. She has never—not once—let me down in all these years that I've been working with her. She is perfect for this type of work, even though she can have a heavy hand.

Work for Love

Take three cleansing baths in a row before starting this work. After your final bath, take a photo of yourself, when your spirit is clean and fresh. Start this work on the fourth day. (The number four is very lucky.)

You will need:

- Ace of hearts
- Ten of hearts
- Nine of hearts
- Four of hearts
- Eight of hearts
- Photo of yourself
- Lavender
- Rose petals
- Lovage root
- Orange peel
- A few teaspoons of dirt from your front and back doors and the four corners of your home

- 1 purple candle
- 3 red candles
- 1 black candle
- Cool glass of water
- Your favorite perfume

Put your dirt in a bowl and add the lavender, rose petals, lovage root, and orange peel. Place the cards on the altar.

Once you have the cards placed—lay them out exactly how I have them written—you will move on to the rest of the work. You will also need a purple candle for Saint Martha to work with on her own, and you need to give her a cool glass of water and a couple sprays of your favorite perfume. You can place these items over to the left side of the altar. You will light her candle and petition her for her help first before you light any of the other candles.

The ace of hearts brings love and happiness; it is placed in the center over your photo.

The ten of hearts is placed on top of the ace of hearts; it counteracts any bad cards that are next to it and brings good luck and success. This is the card that crowns you.

The nine of hearts is placed below the ace. It is the card of satisfaction—the wish card; all your dreams and desires will come true. This is what walks with you.

The four of hearts is placed to the right beside the ace of hearts; this is what you have been carrying with you. You have built walls around your heart and refuse to let changes come through for you.

The eight of hearts is placed to the left; this is the card of movement. Things will final move in the direction you want them too. You are finally moving forward.

Now that you have your cards laid out and you've called on Saint Martha and petitioned her for her help, it is time to finish lighting the rest of the candles. Set down a red candle at the top and a red candle at the bottom; place the black candle to the right and the other red candle to the left. Then you can take your herbal and dirt ingredients and sprinkle them around the foundation, which is the ace of hearts and your photo. Make a closed circle around that candle, the card, and your photo with your ingredients. Now to start the work, usually I would say you light the candles in the order you set them down, but since we have the four of hearts behind you, you are first going to call on Saint Martha and petition her to remove those walls that are blocking and binding you and holding you back from love and success. Light the candle and set it back on top of the card and speak from your heart to Saint Martha so that she may help remove those issues as the candle burns.

Leave this setup as it is. Saint Martha is working. Leave the black candle burning. You will start the rest of the work in the morning when the hands of the clock are going upward.

The next day when you go back to your altar, you will then light the rest of the candles, and you will once again petition Saint Martha on each one of those candles to draw forth the love and success you are looking for. After you petition her, light the candle and repeat the process until all the candles are lit.

You know, you may think, *What, I'm not asking for success; I simply want love.* Darling, you can't have love without success; you can't have love without prosperity. Because if you don't have success *and* prosperity *and* love, then eventually the struggle will destroy the foundation that you are trying to build.

Remember to go daily and say your prayers and your petitions over your work—and don't forget to refresh Saint Martha's water daily as this work is going on.

Once the work is over, you can remove the candles and the card, but take your photo and all the ingredients and tie them up in a handkerchief and hang it over your front door. Refresh the handkerchief once a month by offering it to Saint Martha, along with a purple candle and a cool glass of water. Spray the handkerchief bundle with a little bit of your favorite perfume or cologne.

Once the candle has burned out, you can place the bundle above your front door again, or you can hang it above your bed. The bundle will continue to work as long as you continue feeding it and giving it to Saint Martha for her to keep it filled with power. Remember, the work only works as long as you keep working it; if you're a lazy worker, then your work's not going to last long. Remember, everything costs something.

PEACE AND PROSPERITY WORK

There are times when a home becomes a war zone. You can't find peace anywhere you turn in your own home. This is the time when you need to draw in peace. Here is a small work that can be done in the time of need.

Work for a Peaceful Home

Perform this work as the sun is rising.

You will need:

- A coffee can
- A family photo
- Dirt from the four corners of your home plus the front and back doors
- A pinch of lovage
- A pinch of bloodroot
- A pinch of lavender
- ½ cup sugar
- 1 blue candle

Place your family photo in the coffee can and pour the gathered dirt over it. Add the lovage, bloodroot, and lavender, then pour the sugar on top.

In the wax around the wick of your blue candle, carve the word "peace." Pray Psalm 23 over the candle, and place it in the can with the ingredients. Light the candle. Once the candle burns completely out, displose of it and put the can up for safekeeping.

Repeat the work as needed.

JUSTICE WORK

The scales of justice are a funny thing. So is the sword of justice. When we talk about Conjure work, we say that it is a "justified work," meaning you have to have a good reason before you go after somebody. When doing justice work, you have to make sure that your plate is clean; you have to be sure that you have not done wrong, because you will be hit with that same sword that you are going after your target with.

Justice means just that: getting justice for what was done to you. It doesn't mean going after somebody because you don't like them or they hurt your feelings. Just because they hurt your feelings or make you mad does not mean that you are justified in throwing at them. If you don't like someone, stay away from them, plain and simple.

When I'm talking about justified work, I'm talking about when someone has done you a horrible wrong. A slight is not a wrong; a wrong is when someone has done something to you or yours to cause serious harm. Here is an example. Let's say that you've been on the job for a while. Everything is beautiful, everything is going well, and then all of a sudden they hire somebody new in management. This new person just cannot stand you, even though you never did anything to them. You're just as nice as you can be, but they do not like you. So they decide that they want you off the job. They want to fire you for no good reason even though you've done absolutely nothing wrong. If you decided to go after them, this would be considered a justified work. They attacked you for no reason. They tried to get you fired, which in turn affects your income, which in turn affects your whole life. So, yes, that would be a good reason to do justified work against them.

I'm going to give an example of what is *not* justified work. Let's say you have a neighbor who is always causing issues. They're not necessarily hurting anybody—they just keep things stirred up all the time. Is this a justified work? No. They have done nothing wrong but be annoying and keep things stirred up. You do not have the right to attack them or cross them because they have really done nothing more than act like a donkey.

What you *can* do is (1) freeze them (add their photo and water to a freezer bag and place in the freezer); (2) do a little "shut your mouth" on them (make a "shut your mouth" candle by placing their photo or name on a red candle and burning it); or (3) put them up against the wall (literally nail their photo to the wall, with the image facing the wall). What you should not do is justice work against them. Because being annoying is no reason to send the hounds of hell after them; that would most definitely be an unjustified work.

I'm going to repeat this again: you and you alone are responsible for the works that you do. Once you do a work and it is in the ancestors' hands, then it is out of your control and there is nothing you can do to stop it. So it's always better to think before you move and to not do this type of work when you are angry. If you do an unjustified work against someone and they are smart enough or know enough to do a reversal, you're going to get hit with your own work. That's just the rules of this work; every saying has to be justified. Unjust actions will cause a reaction, and it might not be the one that you want. Just be mindful of the works that you do. I'm not telling you not to do justified work—I do it whenever it's necessary. Just make sure that it is justified. That way you're well protected. And I'm going to throw this in here also: just because you know how to do something doesn't mean you have to do it.

This is a crossing work, so make sure you are justified. If you're not, it can come back on you. This work should be done only in extreme cases of injustice; this is not some light, sugary work. Conjure work is not all about light, love, and happiness. And I'm going to repeat this one more time, and I'm sure you're tired of reading it, but I just want to make sure that you understand: every action causes a reaction and this work should be done only if it is justified.

Work for Justice

You will need:

- Six of clubs
- Four of spades
- Nine of spades
- 2 white candles
- 1 purple candle
- Dirt from three churches
- A photo of the target

To start, place the six of clubs at the top. This is the foundation. This signifies that victory is yours and all problems are being moved out of the way. You have success.

Then place the four of spades underneath and to the left. This signifies jealousy, business troubles, sickness, minor misfortunes, or delays in a project.

Place the nine of spades to the right of the four of spades. This signifies bad luck, delays, quarrels, sleeplessness, sickness, losses, troubles, and family problems.

As you can see, the card that represents your victory is on top of the four of spades and the nine of spades.

Place the purple candle on top of the six of clubs and sprinkle the gathered dirt around the candle and on top of the card. Then place a white candle on each of the other cards.

If you have a photo of the target, place it between the nine of spades and the four of spades.

Light the purple candle first, calling on your ancestors and petitioning them to let victory be yours and justice be served. Pray 2 Chronicles 15:6–7:

> *One nation was being crushed by another and one city by another, because God was troubling them with every kind of distress. But as for you, be strong and do not give up, for your work will be rewarded.*

Remove the white candle from the nine of spades and brush yourself off with it. Then pick up the card and brush yourself off with that. Return your candle and card to their original positions.

If you have a photo of the target, pick it up and brush yourself with it in a reversal or counterclockwise motion. Once you've made three passes from head to toe, put the photo back.

Pick up the four of spades and repeat this process.

Light your candles from right to left. Pray over the two cards and the photo at least three times a day.

You will always pray over the six of clubs first and then move to the other cards. As this work is going, you really need to keep your protections up and keep yourself spiritually cleansed. This is a serious work, so be mindful. Remember that every action causes a reaction. You and you alone are responsible for the works you do, so be sure this work is justified!

Part Three

Other Forms of Divination

READING DEM BONES

Back in the day, many didn't have reading cards, as they cost money—but bones were easily gotten. In addition, bone reading is traditional in Conjure. Reading the bones comes straight out of Africa, although the readings may be a little different The sangomas of South Africa are the traditional bone readers. They are the spiritual doctors and healers, and they take care of their people. Their style of bone reading is different than the one that is worked with over here now, but I feel the concept of our bone reading comes from them and the ancestors that brought it over here through slavery.

We have to understand that when the ancestors were kidnaped and brought across the water, they had absolutely nothing with them except for their knowledge and memories of home. They didn't have notes and books for references; they had stories and information that was handed down by word of mouth from one generation to the next. That is how I have learned everything I know—by word of mouth. That is also the reason I teach the way I do, because that is how I was taught. The ancestors weren't allowed to know how to read and write, although some of them were still taught verbally.

There is a difference in the way the sangomas read the bones and the way I was taught to read the bones. I have been bone throwing since I was a young child. It started out as a game (children learn by what they see and what they hear). I started out with learning the shapes the bones made—a cross, an X, a road, and so on. Then I grew up. I read bones much better than I do cards because the ancestors speak strongly to me through the bones. I think it's because throwing the bones is a traditional way of divining.

The sangomas don't have a limit to the number of bones they have; they keep them in a bowl or basket and throw a handful at a time. They are true healers, so they throw them to find out what is going on with their clients. I know of some people who read sangoma style and swear by it, but that is not a traditional Conjure bone reading.

I have heard some readers say that they have containers of bones and they just grab a handful and throw them out. This is not traditional bone reading. Every reader has a right to read the bones how they want to, but they don't have the right to call it a traditional Conjure bone reading if that is not what it is. Like everything else on the internet, bone reading has become one of the hot topics and everyone is a master. That is one of the main reasons I agreed to write this book—so the foundation won't be lost or turned into something it's not.

I was taught that you should only have enough bones to hold in your hands. This is a rule I have always followed, and it's what I teach. If you have more than that, you might miss something in a throw that could help your client.

As far as I am aware, the ancestors read possum bones, chicken bones, or raccoon bones with extra things added such as roots and other things they found. I think it's important for the knowledge of traditional bone reading to be shared. As elders are passing, so is their knowledge.

Once I got older and began truly reading the bones, I was taught to throw the bones at my client's feet to find out what condition ailed them. You should have a very strong connection with your ancestors. The ancestors speak through the bones; this is how they are able to help you with your daily life. This is truly Conjure at its best; most old-school workers either throw the bones or read playing cards—they don't usually read tarot cards.

GATHERING YOUR BONES

"Where do the bones come from? And how do I get me a set?"

I get asked this question almost every time I finish a bone reading. Traditionally the bones are gathered over time, but in today's fast-paced world most folks just buy them instead of collecting them. My bones have been collected over a span of fifty years or more. I lost my first set—or maybe they were taken from me. Either way, it got gone. The only thing I have left out of it is the piece I was given to move my bones around with, and I only have that because it wasn't in my handkerchief that I kept my bones tied up in—it was on my ancestor altar.

I had to start over. I cured the bones myself just like I was taught to do. Over the years I have found things and have been given things that I have added to them, so I now have a full set again, which I guard with my life. My oldest son and daughter-in-law made me a leather bone bag to keep my bones in about twenty-two years ago, so that is where they stay unless I am working with them. I let very few people handle my bones, as they are linked with my ancestors. I have gifted bones to some of my kids, but it doesn't happen often.

I have things in my bones, including Solomon's seal root for wisdom; Jezebel root for power; a seashell my grandson gave me that represents the flow of spirit in and out, depending on how it falls in the throw; and a turtle that represents prosperity or protection, depending on how it falls.

If you decide to start working with the bones, then you can buy a base set of bones and build from there, or you can take your time and collect your bones. I have a Solomon's seal root in my set that is at least twenty years old and a seashell that my grandson gave me when he was about four years old (he's twenty-five now). You have to remember that our time is not spirit's time, so the bone set may be slow coming or it may just fall into your lap. Either way, collect the pieces with respect and honor because this is how your ancestors will speak to you.

No two bone sets will be the same. No two readers will read the same. The one thing that is very important is that you be able to discern what spirit and the ancestors are trying to convey to you through a reading. It should be what spirit is saying to you and not what you feel like needs to be said. I'm not sure if everybody is gifted for bone reading, but I sure hope they are. This is a skill that is dying out and is being lost. It's worth saving.

I have found that most folks who are meant to read the bones usually started collecting them without even realizing it. Bones just seem to appear or someone will gift them something that could be added and they just hold on to it not really even knowing *why* until one day bone reading comes into their life. No two sets of bones are the same, because no two readers are the same. Your bone set will be unique and very personalized, as it should be.

CREATING YOUR OWN BONE SET

The best way to understand a bone in a reading is to understand the traits of the animal the bone came from. By learning the traits of the animals, you can put the meanings to work in a layout and not have to make shit up. I'm not talking about anybody; I'm just stating the facts. If you are going to throw the bones, then do it right. Understand the animal whose bones you are working with. I'm not saying anybody else is right or wrong; I'm saying use your common sense and think for yourself. If the animal is shady and tricky, then the bones will represent that in a reading. If the animal is loyal or lucky, then their bones will represent that aspect in a reading.

Alligator

The alligator represents balance; it can move between the land and water. The land represents prosperity and growth, while the water represents movement and our emotions. The gator also is powerful and cunning. It will lay in wait to strike its prey. Alligators are resilient; they wait for the right time, and they are sneaky. They represent things that are hidden, but they also represent seeing clearly. They will stew and wait when there is an intruder; they wait for just the right moment to hit their prey. Their duality shows us that they can be protective because of their tough skin and they can see clearly when the waters are murky; but they also represent something that is hidden.

It depends on the other bones around the alligator bone or foot as to the association to the reading. It could mean you have a person who is sneaky, waiting and stewing over the situation, just waiting for the right time to strike; or there could be things hidden from the person who is having the reading done and more information is needed. It could mean that protection is needed or that the person is well protected; it could mean the person has blinders on. If it is around money, then this could go two ways: either the movement is going toward success and prosperity or you have a cunning person who is trying to rip you off.

Armadillo

The armadillo is known for its hard, protective shell. They are a bit self-centered, as their safety comes first. They love to dig, and they are very good at finding things. They are also good at hiding because they can close themselves up in their protective shell. They will drop and roll into a ball. They are persistent; they will keep digging until they find that root or worm they're after. If this bone represents a person in the reading, then that person will be persistent, think only of themselves, and be nosy. Since we know that the armadillo is all about protection, then the client might need some strong protection work.

They may have a hidden enemy who is determined. Like the armadillo, this enemy will be persistent, and it is probably someone in the client's circle. The armadillo needs a lot of sleep and is only awake about six hours a day. They are slow movers, so don't expect them to move fast. Any project or anything the client is trying to do will likewise be slow moving. Nothing is going to get done in that little bit of time. So this bone will always represent very slow movement.

Black Cat

Black cat bones are lucky, period. The cat is a supernatural animal; they are graceful, mysterious, clever, secretive, and watchful. They are very selective in who they choose to trust and are very independent. They are also protective and will attack when they feel threatened. If the bones fell just right and this bone represents a person, then this person is likely very private in their lives; they are watchful of the folks around them, and they may also have a strong second sight. It could also represent someone who is really clever, secretive, and sneaky who is just waiting for the right time to pounce. Cats are known to see spirits, so the bones falling in the right spot in the reading could mean a spirit that walks with you is trying to give you a message or ask for something.

Buzzard

The buzzard flies effortlessly through the air, letting the current pull him along. It will circle its prey for hours at a time, going around and around just gliding on air currents. It is very patient. The buzzard eats dead things, plain and simple. It will clean the meat right off the bone. If this bone comes up in a reading, I'd say some serious cleansing work needs to be done, depending on how the other bones fall. If the question is about a situation, then I would say that the client needs to be patient and bide their time. All good things come to those who wait.

Chicken

They aren't a primary part of my set, but chicken bones are traditional for a bone throwing set. The chicken is always digging and scratching, constantly cleaning its yard or space. It is always aware of what is going on around it, and it is very good at defending its space. By nature, the chicken likes its freedom and doesn't like to be caged up. It likes to roam around the yard. Chickens get along well with other chickens in the yard, but they don't like intruders. The one thing about the chicken is that most of the time if it rambles off it will come back home. Ever heard the old saying, "Come home to roost"?

I grew up around chickens. They are good alarm systems, as they are always on the lookout for danger. They will also let you know when a storm is brewing. Chickens lay eggs, which feed us and bring prosperity if you sell them.

They are also very fertile. It depends on the other bones in the reading, but if the chicken bone comes up near the one you are reading for it could mean a few things. Your client may need a strong cleansing and protection. They may be in danger. If the question was one about love, then the person may not be good for them; they may represent the danger in the reading and they will probably be one of those folks who rambles all the time and is only around to eat, sleep, and have sex, then they are off again hanging out. If the reading is about prosperity, then I would say that the client will have plenty, but they need to do a little protection work around their money.

Coon

Raccoon bones are also traditional Conjure throwing bones. The coon is very intelligent. It's excellent at solving puzzles, and will steal bait off traps. Coons can be both appealing and devious; they are greedy and have a hearty appetite. They are also charming. They are flexible; they have more than one home and find it hard to stay in one place. They are vagabonds by nature. Male coons are only interested in the family during mating season, but the female stays with the family throughout. A coon is happy to share unless the supply is limited—then it becomes territorial. Of course, we know the coon penis bone represents love. But what about a regular coon bone?

If the reading is about love and a man is involved and this bone falls in the right place, I'd say run as fast as you can. This guy is not interested in a relationship; he's interested in what he can get at the moment. Even though he may seem perfect and lovable, he is tricky and underhanded. If it has to do with business deals or money, then I would say you need to find another way because the person you are dealing with is underhanded and devious even though he may seem charming and giving. This person will move on and leave you holding the bag.

If this reading is concerning a woman, I'd say she is a good woman and will be faithful; she will keep the home fire burning. It really all depends on the question and the other bones around this one. I would do another throw if this bone is near the person I am reading for just to make sure I see the whole picture.

Coyote

The coyote is known as the "trickster." This bone represents underhandedness, and your being tricked by someone—a person who can't be trusted. Watch your back; the coyote is very cunning and selfish. If you are using a coyote back bone or tail bone and it comes up in a reading, this doesn't mean the client is going to have back problems; it means someone is going to stab them in the back—someone they trusted. In most Native American stories the coyote represents a male, but it can also represent a female. This person is a survivalist and will do whatever they have to do to survive. The coyote represents a person (male or female) who never has enough, and always wants more. It could also mean underhandedness in business or a competitor using tricks against you.

Deer

The deer is graceful, peaceful, and swift. It is very watchful and aware of what is going on around them. It always finds the abundance of food in the wild, so it represents abundance and success. If this bone comes up in a reading it could represent a person of peace who also moves with swiftness to solve problems. It can also mean that money issues are over and success is at hand, or that a job is moving with the swiftness of the deer. It could mean to be watchful and keep an eye out for trouble.

Dog

Some claim that the dog bone can represent loyalty, as we know the dog is man's best friend. This is kind of one-sided thinking, though, because not all dogs are sweet and lovable. Some can be downright viscous. Dogs are also territorial and defensive when it comes to their yard. They are also very protective when it comes to their owners. If you are going to work with a dog bone in your set, then you need to look at the whole picture, not just one side of it. If you do a bone throw and the dog bone lands next to you but the whole feel of the reading and the other bones around the dog bone tell you danger is near, I wouldn't take that to mean someone is being loyal. I would take it to mean I need to get my defenses up; I need to protect my space and myself.

Fox

The fox is sometimes seen as a messenger who is noble and wise. But on the other hand, depending on whom you ask, the fox is seen as cunning and sly. Have you ever heard the old saying, "He's as sly as a fox"? The fox is very tricky and clever. It is quick-thinking, and can adapt because it has strong wisdom. Foxes also like playing games, and they can lead you into danger if you don't watch your step. I think the spirit of the fox is a multiple personality that can be whatever is needed at that moment.

This bone could have a couple of different meanings in a reading. It could represent someone who is wise and noble; someone who is there to help you. Or a message of great wisdom is coming your way. The bone in the reading next to the client could mean someone they are dealing with is underhanded, that they are leading the person in the wrong direction that could cause them a lot of trouble. If it is near the bone that represents money, then it could mean the client is going to lose their money. It could also mean that the person they are dealing with is tricky, sly, and is playing games. If the reading is concerning love or money, I'd advise my client to drop this person like a hot tator. This person can change to suit the situation, and caution should always be used when dealing with this person. I would advise a deeper reading if this bone comes near the client.

Goat

The goat can be tricky. Sometimes it may seem mild-mannered or shy. You may even think that it is just a dumb beast. But don't be fooled. If you have ever watched goats in the field, you will notice that one minute everything is fine and the next they may try to headbutt you. They are strong-minded and will just keep coming at you. They don't usually try to get out of their fenced in areas because they are happy to just stay in their own space. If this bone comes up in a reading and represents a person, then I would have to say that the person in question is stubborn and won't give up easily. I would also go as far as to say they could be very clever and tricky if there was a need for it. They prefer to be on their own territory rather than someone else's and will strike when you least expect it. I would use caution when dealing with this person, and I would also look deeper into the reading.

Hawk

The hawk represents letting go, being free, and not holding yourself back. It also tells when it is time to be still. In other words, stop, look, and listen; something may be a bit wrong. The hawk is alert and sees all. So if this claw came up in a reading, it could represent a secret being told, or someone being found out. The hawk also brings messages and represents change. If the hawk claw falls near the target in a reading, it could mean the target is unsure, that they are holding themselves back.

Possum

The possum's hind legs look like human hands, so that may be one reason their bones are traditional for throwing. The possum is well known for playing dead as a means of defense. The possum doesn't want to fight, so it always has a backup plan. It can be very tricky. Things are never the way they seem with the possum; it is the master of deception. Possums are well known as nature's Conjurers. Some folks think of the possum as being nasty, but truth be told they keep themselves as clean as a house cat does. They like to be in the dark and quiet. It is wise and is good at uncovering things.

If this bone came up in a love or money reading, I would say there is some major deception going on and nothing is what it seems. If it came up in a general reading, then I would say the person has issues: They like being alone, they are deceptive and not telling the truth. They are hiding something from the reader or they are blind to something that is going on around them. It really depends on where it falls in a reading and what the question is; but like the possum, the bone represents deception, blindness, someone who always comes out clean in any mess they may dig into. The possum has the wisdom to find out the truth.

Rabbit

Rabbits are generally calm and laid-back. They will let you hold them and are lovable—but they do have their limits. Some folks may say that rabbits are timid, but I think they are just wise and wait to see how things are going to go before they react. They don't go rushing into anything. Everyone knows that rabbits are very sexual, and I'm not sure they stick with one mate for life. If this bone represented a person in a reading, it could represent a person who spreads themselves around; someone who may not be faithful but is lovable and caring. They will be patient and work toward what they want. When they are pushed, they will push back. If you are in a relationship with this type of person, I would caution you to stay on top of your business and know what they are doing.

Rat

Rats can adapt to almost any environment, and they are great at avoiding traps. They are cunning and shrewd, and will defend themselves when they have too. They are also nervous and jumpy. They have a built-in foresight—that is why you see them jumping from sinking ships or burning buildings. Rats are survivors; they will save themselves above all else. They can also adjust to any situation. You have to remember that the rat will find a way into any stronghold. Nothing is safe with them, because they never get full, they never have enough, and they want it all. They are very good at hiding and waiting for the right time to get what they want. In a reading, I would look at this person as someone who is calculating and will do whatever they have to in order to succeed. They will bide their time. This bone represents underhandedness at its best because the rat will change when change is needed to fit in. Watch the reading closely if this bone falls near the person you are reading for.

Snake

The snake is like a double-edged sword; it can represent good luck or bad luck. A snake sheds its old skin and transforms into the new. The snake also waits in hiding for the right time to strike its prey. Its venom can kill, so it's not all light and sweet. The snake is not all about healing and doing away with the old. The snake represents things that are hidden, and unknown enemies.

It will depend on how the other bones fall as to the interpretation of the snake vertebra. You will have to double-check the reading because the meanings could be so different. The bone could mean the person having the reading is going through a big transformation, things could finally be moving in the right direction, or a healing is coming. The other side of this same coin is like that ole saying, "There's a snake in the grass somewhere!" The bone can also represent hidden enemies, spitefulness, attack, betrayal, and a person who can change their skin at will, who can become whatever they need to become. It also represents fast change or an enemy striking fast. You will have to be the judge of which meaning the bone represents in your reading. I'll give you a little sage advice: double-check the reading, because this bone can represent danger.

Turkey

The turkey struts and preens around the yard, showing himself off, while the mama hustles around the young or is busy building the nest. Turkeys are constantly pecking and scratching, looking for food. They love roosting high in trees out of sight. The turkey is well known to gobble things up and is known as a gobbler. So they are wonderful for cleansings and eating things up. If this bone represented a person in the reading, then I would say they are all about family and can get their hustle on to achieve their goals. They may also put themselves on a lofty perch to watch and see what is going on around them. This bone could also be an alert to danger and represent a need for a cleansing.

Wolf

The wolf is very intelligent and loyal; it mates for life. Wolves take care of their pack members. They are compassionate and affectionate, and they have great communication skills and strong bonds with their pack. Wolves don't like fighting; they will try to avoid aggression and conflict if possible. In other words, they prefer to walk away. If walking away is not an option, then they will stand their ground.

The wolf is misunderstood. It is cunning and may find another solution to a problem. This doesn't mean the wolf is underhanded; it just means it is smarter than the average Joe. The person this bone represents is compassionate, intelligent, loyal, cunning, and a great communicator, and they will stand their ground if they have to, but they prefer peace.

Skeleton Key

A skeleton key will open all doors; it fits every lock. If the key falls near the person the reading is being done for it can mean two things, depending on the other bones in the reading: it could mean that your roads are already open or that you need to do some road opening work. If the key is pointing upward, then I would say to move forward with whatever project you have going on. If the key is facing downward, then I would say that you need to do some cleansing, and you might want to rethink your plan. Again, it really all depends on how the other bones in the reading fall. Always use your common sense and listen to your spirits when they speak to you.

DEDICATING YOUR BONES

Once you have collected your bones, it is time to cleanse and dedicate them to the ancestors. Let's talk about cleansing them first. You will need to fill a basin with a wash made of bay leaves, salt, and baking soda.

Rinse your bones off with cool running water and then add them to the basin. Say a prayer over them as you move them around in the wash. Lay out a towel and remove the bones from the wash and let them air dry on a white handkerchief. Once they are dry, dress them with holy oil. Then it is time to offer them up to your ancestors.

You will need:

- A large white handkerchief
- Your bones
- 5 white seven-day candles
- A cool glass of water
- 1 purple seven-day candle
- Spiritual oil

Make sure that you have done a cleansing before you start this work. It's important for you to be spiritually cleansed because you do not want anything that shouldn't be there getting into your bones. Once you have everything ready, lay out the white handkerchief and spread your bones out on top of it. Then, working with one bone at a time, pick up each bone and blow three breaths over it. Then set it back in its place. Do this with each bone until you have blown life into all of them.

Place one of your white candles in the center of the bones, then place one at the top, one at the bottom, one to the right, and one to the left. Place the glass of water on the right-hand side, and the purple candle on the left-hand side. When you're done, you should have your bones in the center of a cross, with a candle in the center of the bones.

Now that you have everything set up, it is time to call on the ancestors and petition them to fill your bones with their power and their discernment, so you will be able to read for anyone who comes to you for a reading. Tap the purple candle three times on the altar, then call on your ancestors and tell them that the candle is there for them to have something to work with while they fill your bones with their power. Light the candle.

Next, pick up the glass of water and call on your ancestors and offer it to them. Tell them you're giving them the glass of water to quench their thirst. Then set the water back where it goes.

You're going to then light the candles in the order that you set them down. Light the first candle, call on your ancestors, and say your prayer and your petition for them to fill your bones with their power so you will be able to understand whatever it is that they are trying to tell you during a reading. Light the bottom candle and repeat the prayers and petitions. Light the candle to the right and then light the candle to the left. Pick up the candle that is in the center of your bones and hold it up to your mouth and say your prayer and your petition into it. The center candle is the one that is going to feed the bones light. Set the candle back in the center and light it.

Go back at least three times a day and say your prayer and your petitions over your bones. You should keep this going for at least twenty-one days.

Once the twenty-one days are up, wrap your bones in the handkerchief and place them under your pillow for another seven days. On the seventh day, take the bones out. Blow three breaths over your bones. Pick them up in your hands and gently drop them on your handkerchief. Don't try too hard; just sit there quietly and look at them. Try to understand what the bones are saying.

Once you are finished, wrap them up and put them back under your pillow for seven more days. Repeat the process until the bones have been under your pillow for a period of twenty-one days. You are going to have to build a connection between you and your bones. The only way to do this is to work with them: ask them questions that you already know the answer to, then throw them. Sit quietly and study the pattern of the throw. See if you can read them and understand the message and wisdom they are sharing. The one thing that you cannot do is get nervous and not trust your own intuition, because to not trust yourself is to not trust your ancestors. You got this!

EASY-TO-UNDERSTAND BONES

When I started trying to teach folks how to read the bones, I came up with color-coding the bones. This is not how I learned to read the bones, but I thought it would be an easy way to teach. Each bone can be color-coded so it is easily recognized; but you need to be able to communicate with your ancestors so you will get a clear understanding and a clear picture of what the layout is telling you. I know a lot of folks don't honor their ancestors—not because they don't want to, but because they don't know how. It's important that you build that connection so you will be able to interpret the patterns the bones make in the reading. Bone reading is basically like building a puzzle.

You as the reader have to find out how the different bones fit together to tell the story. It might not make sense at first; you may even feel a little confused the first few times you throw the bones. Be patient with yourself. Bone reading is not something you can learn overnight. It's a process that requires a lot of patience; it also requires a strong relationship with your ancestors. You will need to develop this skill so you can learn to discern what spirit is really saying to you. This is what makes a true bone reader different from someone who is making things up as they go along. If you dedicate your bones, you will learn to follow spirit and not worry so much about the meanings of the bones.

You start by connecting all the puzzle pieces. When you can do this, then the picture will become clearer. You have to keep pushing at it, and before you know it the whole puzzle is completed. Bone reading works the same way as putting that puzzle together. Each bone tells its own unique story. The thing to remember is to relax and let spirit guide you in the reading. Once you learn as a reader how the different bones relate to one another and learn to read the pattern of the bones and also listen to spirit and discern what they are telling you, then you'll know how to read for a client even if they try to hide something from you. The bones will tell it.

As I said at the start, this is a system I started for my students; this is not how I was taught. I wasn't lucky enough to have marked bones to help guide me, and even though the system is different, the foundation is the same. The only thing I have changed is that I mark the bones so it's easier to read them. As long as the foundation that my elders gave me in bone reading is intact, then this is a traditional Conjure bone reading book. Like I said, there is not another one like it.

I do want to say this before we move on with the lessons. Nothing is written in stone; if you throw the bones and one of them looks like a snake, then it's a snake! It doesn't matter if it's a bone that represents love; if that came up in a reading, I would say the person having the reading done had a cheater on their hands. This is just a guide to help you build a strong foundation between you, your ancestors, and your bones so you can be the best reader you can be. No one can tell you what spirit is telling you except you; you know what you feel and see. So, with that said, no one can tell you how to read the bones—but they can guide you, and that is what I am trying to do with this book.

INTERPRETING THE READING

You must be relaxed when you throw the bones for the first time. If you followed the instructions on how to prepare your bones, then you should have a good connection with them and your ancestors already. The main thing that you need to remember is to read the layout in sections and to trust in yourself. If you try to read the whole thing at once it might not make sense to you. I have been reading bones for many years—before most folks even knew what bone reading was—and I still read the way I was taught: one section at the time.

Most folks didn't even know what bone reading was until it was put out there on a few popular websites. Then everyone became a bone reader (or did they?). There's not much information out there on how to really read the bones. Bone reading is really something that should be taught hands-on, but it's hard to find a mentor and everyone is so busy nowadays. It takes years to really understand how to interpret what spirit is trying to get across to the reader. Even I'm still learning. It also takes a lot of dedication—not only to the ancestors but also to the bones, because without practice you are wasting your time. You need to have a firm foundation built with your ancestors and the spirits that walk with you. This is a must. Bone reading is a gift from spirit, and folks who come to you for a reading depend on you to be able to hear what the ancestors and spirits are saying through the bones. Like my granddaughter tells me, "Go big or go home!" In plain English: If you can't give it your all, don't do it!

When you throw the bones, you should pay close attention to how they are grouped. Look closely at each bone and how it is lying next to the other bones. This is important because it can tell of blocks or other issues that are going on. I always look for the client's bone first, and then start from there most of the time. But sometimes an area in the throw will catch my eye and I will start there. I don't start the reading the same way every time, but I always look for the client's bone first.

Every reading should start with one question. If there are too many questions asked at once it's hard to read—you will be looking all over the layout for all the answers. So, if the question is about finances, then that is where you start the reading. Of course, you can read your layout any way you want to, but this way makes sense and is how I was taught as a young reader.

I don't have a PhD, but there are one or two things I do know, and that is southern Conjure work and bone reading. True bone readers are far and few nowadays because all the ole folks are dying off. That is one of the main reasons I wanted to add bone reading to this book. I am going to try to explain to you in an easy-to-understand way because I usually teach hands-on when I am teaching a bone-reading class, but I feel everyone should be able to read the bones if they feel called to, so I will try to be as clear as possible.

The first thing I do is brush myself off or rub myself down with some type of spiritual water or holy oil. This clears my spirit and gets me in the right frame of mind to read.

Then I lay out my bones (unless I have already been reading them—then they would be out on my deerskin). I pick up the bones and blow three cleansing breaths on them in between clients. This keeps them clean and keeps my spirit with them.

Once I have the client sitting in front of me and I have blown my three breaths over the bones to cleanse them, I shuffle them around and hold them out to the client. Now they will blow three breaths over the bones and say their own name three times over them. I was taught that this links the bones to the client that I am reading for until the reading is over. Next, I'll drop the bones gently on my deerskin. I don't touch the bones right away. I will sit there and look at them and pray for spirit to show me which section to start at. I usually look for the man or the woman dolly that I have in the bone set to represent a male and a female to see where they have fallen in the throw. Once I find where they have landed in the throw I will look around and see where the other pieces have fallen and what type of story unfolds. I always ask the client for a question, what it is they're looking for. Nobody wants to have a bone reading just to have one—everyone is looking for something if they're getting any type of reading.

If the client tells me they'll have a question after I throw the bones, I'll tell them that I don't do dry readings. As a reader, you need somewhere to start. For me, dry readings are disrespectful to not only my ancestors but also the spirits that walk with me. Anytime I throw the bones or lay out the cards, I am petitioning my spirits to come and help me understand what I am seeing. This is not a game to them or to me. Folks always have a reason for wanting a reading. They may not think that it's important enough to ask the question, but anytime a client sits down at your table for a reading, any question that they ask should be important to you as a reader.

It's your job to listen to the client and to give them the best reading possible.

Reading the bones is truly one of the best readings you will be able to give your client. I say this because the information you will be receiving is coming straight from your ancestors and the spirits that walk with you; you cannot go wrong. That's why it's so important for you to have a strong connection with not only your bones but also the spirits who will be connecting with you through the reading.

Once I find my starting point within the reading, I will talk with the client and tell them what I see. Most of the time they're shocked that I can see so much information about them simply through the bones, and I always explain that it's not me—spirit is talking.

When the reading is over, I put a spiritual wash in my hands and shuffle my bones around while praying that they be cleansed. Using the same wash, I do a brush down on myself to clear away any residue from the reading.

I then take a little bit of fiery wall of protection oil (see below) in the palm of my hands and rub my hands briskly together. Then I shuffle the bones and try to get a light coat of oil on each one of them. I do this after each reading to clean and clear my bones.

FIERY WALL OF PROTECTION OIL

This is a powerful tool that offers protection from crossed conditions.

You will need:

- 3 olive leaves
- 3 pieces of Frankincense
- 1 small piece of dried red pepper
- 1 bottle olive oil

Pray over each ingredient before adding to a base olive oil. Once all ingredients have been added, pray Psalm 23 into the bottle of oil. This turns it into holy oil.

BONE THROWING Q&A

Q: Does it matter what type of bones I use?

A: I was taught to throw possum or raccoon bones; but I do know some ole workers who like to throw chicken bones. So I guess the answer to the question is no, I don't think it matters. Possum, coon, and chicken bones are traditional within Conjure. It all depends on the reader, I think. I try not to set rules for other folks; I just try to guide them in the right direction.

Q: What if two bones cross?

A: There are times when two bones cross each other. This is not always a bad thing. It all depends on what the bones represent. If the bone representing the client falls across the bone that represents a cross condition, then I would take that as a good sign. Now, if it were the other way around, that wouldn't be good at all.

Q: How many bones can I have in my set?

A: There are lots of different answers to this, but I was taught that a set should have no fewer than thirteen bones and no more than twenty-one.

Q: Do I feed the bones?

A: I was taught that the bones should be cleansed and fed once a month if you work with them a lot. You can set them on a layer of salt for twenty-four hours, then dress them with holy oil, pray over them, and give them to your ancestors for twenty-four hours. This will not only cleanse them but also empower them.

Q: How many times should I throw the bones in a reading?

A: I was taught to throw the bones one to three times. This is not written in stone; it isn't a law or anything. I hardly ever have to throw the bones three times. There have been times when they have spoken so clearly to me that once was enough. It depends on the reading and the situation that is being looked into. If the client has more than one question, then I throw on each question.

Q: What happens if the bones keep saying the same thing?

A: If you throw the bones three times and you keep getting the same answer, then they are not going to tell you anything else. (The cards will do the same thing, because until something changes, the cards will continue to repeat the same or near same layout.) If this happens, then either stop the reading or ask another question. Don't ask the same question worded a different way; ask something completely different.

Q: What if a bone falls off the cloth?

A: There will be times when you throw the bones and one or more of them rolls off the handkerchief. Don't pick them up and put them back with the others. Look at the whole layout first; see if it makes sense. Most of the time something is being moved away, or it could be that bone doesn't have a place in the reading.

Q: Should I cleanse before and after a reading?

A: Yes. You should always cleanse your bones before and after a reading. You don't want to bring parts of an old reading into a new one. That would be like making a peanut butter and jelly sandwich on stale bread.

Q: Do I have to throw my bones on the dirt?

A: No. In some areas it may be taught to throw them on the dirt, but I was taught to throw them at my client's feet while they stood on a white sheet. I'm not sure if white was used because it's holy or if it was because that's all they had back in the day.

Q: Can I give my bones to a saint or a spirit?

A: I'm going to step out on a limb here and say flat out no! The bones are a way for your ancestors to help you find answers to the questions you are seeking. The bones should be dedicated to your ancestors because they speak through them. I never tell folks how to do their work because it is *their work,* but here I have to say the bones must be given to your ancestors.

Q: If the bones make shapes, does that mean something?

A: Sometimes the bones will make shapes. One time I was doing a reading for a client who was having issues getting their life to move forward. We did some work to help the process, then a while later I threw the bones to see if we were headed in the right direction. The bone that represented my client was at the end of what looked to me like an open road; everything else was left behind. So that was my answer. Yes, the work had worked, and the roads to success were opened.

Q: Can I combine my bone reading with a card reading?

A: Yes. I do this when I am working on something but I can't seem to get a straight answer or I feel like something is missing.

Q: Can others touch my bones?

A: Yes. I have never been one of those readers who thought if someone touched my tools they wouldn't work anymore. I want my clients to touch the tools so they can pick up on spirit and I can get a good reading. Just be sure to cleanse the bones or other tools afterward, so avoid crossing signals.

Q: Can I move the bones around during a reading?

A: Yes, you can move the bones around. As a young reader I was taught not to touch the bones during a reading. I was given a shell to move them around with. But as I have gotten older I sometimes will move them around with my finger.

Q: What if I just don't understand what the bones are trying to tell me?

A: If you throw the bones and for whatever reason you just can't seem to understand what they are trying to tell you, then call on your ancestors for help. Gather up your bones and hold them up to your mouth. Petition your ancestors to help you understand what the bones are saying. Then re-throw the bones. If you still don't understand what they are saying to you, wrap them up and place them on your ancestor altar for three days. Go daily and petition your ancestors to speak to you clearly, in a way you understand.

Now you should have some kind of idea on how to interpret the different bones from the different animals in a reading. You have to remember to look at the whole picture and not just a section. Most importantly, listen to your ancestors and your spirits that walk with you. Remember too that you are not always going to see the same picture as another reader, because each person is unique. Don't try to be like Mike! Be you, and follow your own spirits; they will always read true for you. This book is a guide to help you find your way, not a law.

BLUE WATER

I grew up with blue water. When I was growing up, all the nurses had to wear white, so bluing was sold in every store. Blue water was a big thing back in the day, and the bluing was easy to get. I have noticed that nowadays there isn't a lot of blue water being worked with. I think that this is because folks don't really know what to do with it. The most you see said about blue water is that it can be added to a bath or it can be worked with for protection. I remember seeing my mama sitting at the kitchen table with a jar of blue water in front of her. She didn't read the cards that I know of, but she looked into that jar of water.

Blue water is very good for protection and for clearing out unwanted things in the home. I am going to share a small setup that I was taught to do every time I changed or refilled my jar of water. For those of you who might not know, blue water is excellent for divination; not only does it offer protection while you are doing your consultation, but it also acts like a crystal ball. Blue water can be worked with just like you would any sightseeing tool. I want to share with you not only how to make blue water but also how to see into it.

BLESSED BLUING WATER

You need a clean glass or jar, to start. I always use an old mason jar because that's what I saw my mama use, but you can work with whatever type of container you would like. You need to get your bluing. You can find Mrs. Stewart's Bluing in the cleaning/laundry aisle of the grocery store. It only costs a few dollars for a 16-ounce bottle, which will last a very long time—a little bit goes a long way. You can also add a cupful to your whites to bless your clothes as you do the laundry.

You will need:

- 1 teaspoon table salt
- 1 teaspoon baking soda
- 1 teaspoon Epsom salt
- Mrs. Stewart's Bluing

Base Water

First, you'll make your base: I make mine in my copper pot, but you can use whatever type of pot you have. Place a half gallon of water in a large pot on the stove and turn the burner to high. When the water starts the boil, add your ingredients, turn the fire down to low, and stir while you pray Psalm 23 at least three times. Once the salt has dissolved, turn the fire off and set the pot aside to cool.

With a marker, write the date and the name of the contents on your storage container (I use a half-gallon mason jar). Make sure your container has been washed and spiritually cleansed before you pour your base into it. I prefer to use a glass container rather than a plastic one, but I grew up in a time when there were only glass containers for milk and such. Pour your base into the jar and store it in a cool, dark place. This will keep it from going bad.

Multipurpose Blue Water

When you are ready to make a batch of blue water, simply drop three drops of bluing into your glass of water. I use the blade of my knife to stir the bluing into the water if the water is going to be worked with for cut and clear and protection. Once you have your water mixed, set your glass or jar on a white handkerchief and then make a circle around the jar with a few tea lights, starting at the top then moving to the left and working your way around until you reach the first candle set down. Once you have the circle made, you light the tea lights in the order you set them down, speaking your petition and prayer for protection and cut and clear. Let the tea lights burn completely out before you start to work with the water. This water can be put into a spray bottle, a bath, or a mop bucket.

READING TABLE BLUE WATER

If you're making blue water for your reading table, the process is basically the same, but with a couple changes. As the water begins to boil, pray Psalm 23 and Isaiah 11:2, which says:

> *And the spirit of the Lord shall rest upon him, the spirit of wisdom and understanding, the spirit of counsel and might, the spirit of knowledge and of the fear of the Lord.*

Follow the same steps as above, and as you add the bluing, repeat Isaiah 11:2.

Lay out a white handkerchief, set your blue water in the center of it, and get four tea lights. You are going to set the tea lights in a cross setup, starting at the top one, then the bottom, then the left and the right. Light the tea lights in the order you set them down, praying Isaiah 11:2 over each one. Bend over where your breath can blow into your container of blue water and repeat the prayer three times while letting your breath flow over the container. Let the tea lights burn down completely. Then your blue water is ready to be looked into.

I always keep a jar of blue water on my reading table along with a white candle that I keep going all the time. Sometimes I will let my reading water dry completely before I put in fresh water, but if I have a difficult reading then I will pour the water out and add fresh water and repeat the prayers all over again. It really just depends on what's going on.

This is an old way to make spiritual water that is powerful and filled with prayer. You notice I did not say this is the *only* way; I'm sure there are others who make their water differently. I have found over the years that by keeping this water on my reading table it really helps the readings and the way I interact with my clients. As always, use what works for you.

THE CANDLE SPEAKS

I became infatuated with candles when I was in elementary school. We had a teacher, Ms. Hall, who was really different from all the other teachers in the school. I am now convinced that she was a practicing witch. She wore all these flowing skirts because back then women were not allowed to wear pants to school. Even the teachers were not allowed. She always wore a lot of heavy jewelry and had the coolest glasses I have ever seen. She taught our class how to make candles out of a gulf wax, crayons, and cotton twine. We made our candles in tin cans. She also taught us how to crochet. Even though I was young I have never forgotten her. That was the first time I ever saw anyone make a stick candle with cotton string and wax. We were not allowed to dip the string in the wax, but she showed us how it was done. We did, however, get to pour our wax in our cans to make our candles with her help. I think that this was truly my first step to making candles and burning candles.

When I was young, my aunt took me to the Catholic Church with her without my mama knowing it. I'm not sure if it was from all the candles and incense or from spirit, but I passed out in church. My aunt didn't have a choice but to tell my mama that she had taken me to the Catholic Church without asking. My mama had a fit. I was never allowed to go back to the Catholic Church as long as I lived at home. When I left home, I became a Catholic. Of course, my mama was not real happy about that. That is when I started learning about the saints. Then I had my oldest boy, who is forty-six now. He was sick with asthma and was in and out of the hospital all the time. I was a young mother and really didn't know what I was doing. His ole padrino taught me how to do cleansings working with candles, herbs, and prayers, and I have been doing it ever since. So candle burning is a big part of my work.

CANDLE LOADING

Back in the seventies there weren't a whole lot of glass candles like there are today. I made my own stick candles by dipping cotton string into wax. I have worked with candles since the seventies. When I was first starting out I learned to work with stick candles. I like them because you can mark on them and you can also dress them with oil then roll them in herbs before you light them. I don't think that one is better than the other; it all depends on what you have been taught and what you prefer.

I used to hand-dip my own stick candles. I still do sometimes, if I have a real important job I need to do or some serious cleansing or block-busting work. Hand-dipping the candle is really the best way to go because you can roll it in roots and herbs as you are making it. You can also burn photos to ash and add that to the candle as you make it. Prayers can be prayed over and over with every dip into the wax. Dipping your own candles makes some powerful works.

The good thing about dipping your own candles is that you can roll them in a Conjure powder while they're still wet. We called this "loading." This is truly old-school Conjure work. Back in the day there was not a lot of adding all the things that are being added today. It was simply string, wax, ash, and whatever else you were going to load the candle with. It was easy to read the wax back then because you didn't have a lot of oil and dried herbs loaded into the candle. Those things can cause the candle to catch on fire and also cause the candle to go out if it's overloaded. I know folks do things differently nowadays, but truly the old way is the best way if you are going to get a true read from the wax.

There is an art to candle burning and being able to read the wax and truly know how the candle is burning. I feel like if you are going to be burning candles you need to have some idea of what it means when the flame goes out or there's too much wax left—these things are important. I truly don't think that there is a right way or one way to do this, and I say this because the true interpretation comes from spirit. It doesn't matter if it's reading the wax of a candle, looking in blue water, or working with a pendulum; it all comes from the ancestors and from spirit.

Finally, you should always do some type of divination before you ever light a candle. Spirit should always be consulted, because you may not even need to light a candle—you may, in fact, not need to do anything. This is an important habit that you should start if you are going to be doing any type of spiritual work.

WHERE TO START

I prefer not to waste my time doing a work that will not be a success or have the possibility of failing because I didn't take the time to get myself together before I started the job. I have found over the years that taking the time to get myself set up before I start not only saves me time, but it also saves me money. I try to do it the right way the first time. I know in today's world everyone is busy and there is barely enough time to think, but if you are going to do a candle burn I'm sure you want it to be a success.

I'm going to share some of my secrets and some of the reasons my works seem to work so well. The first thing you should do before starting any type of spiritual work is some type of divination; the reason for this is to see if you are doing the right work or if the work is even needed. If things have been off or seem to be going all wrong, I would do a cleansing before ever laying out a card or working with my pendulum. If you have all this stuff going on you probably will not get a clear reading, or you might not understand what you are being told, and discernment is needed in this type of work.

Even if life is full of bliss and happiness and the cards or pendulum say to go for the burn I would do at least a quick brush down before I started any type of burn. Here's the reason why: In our daily lives we are around all types of folks; some of them may cause stress or they may not have our best interest at heart. You do not want to carry that into any candle work—or any type of spiritual work, for that matter. It is always best to start out fresh.

After the brush down, I will lay out the cards or work with my pendulum to try to find out what are the best steps for me to take moving forward. I have little tricks I use when I start a job. If the job is to draw something or someone, I will always start that type of work when the hands of the clock are moving upward. If it's a job for me to remove something, then I will start that work when the hands of the clock are moving downward. For me, it is important to start the burn at the right time.

I always keep detailed notes on my candle burns, including any sudden changes. This is important so you can keep track of how things go after the burn. I also take photos of my burns throughout, as a way to keep track of any changes in the flame. If something weird starts happening, like a lot of noise or a lot of movement, I will do a divination to see exactly what is going on. Make sure you note the day, the time, and how the burn is going, as well as how you are feeling—especially if it is cleansing or healing work.

This may seem like a lot of work for one candle burn, but if you do it every time it will become a habit and you will learn the feel of a candle burn. If the flame is low, or has a lot of movement, or makes a lot of noise, you will notice it; all these things can help you.

CLEANSING A CANDLE

I know nowadays folks don't have time to make their own candles. In the days when I first started out as a worker, it was the best way to get candles. But today you can find candles in every store you go into. Even if they are not made for spiritual works, they can still be worked with—you simply have to do a little extra work to them.

Before you do any type of work with a candle, you should clean it first. I mean, think about it. That candle has probably sat on a store shelf for who knows how long. How many folks have picked it up and looked at it? I believe candles hold a memory; they pick up our feelings. If someone who is depressed or down and out picked up the candle before you, then I believe some of those feelings got on the candle. Or how about someone who is very angry? The first thing you need to remember is that you are not the only one in the store looking for candles. Therefore, you are not the only one picking them up and looking at them. Not everyone has a clean spirit on them. Some folks carry the spirit of envy, jealousy, hatred, and God only knows what else. Then there are those folks who have such a negative spirit about them you can almost taste it when you are around them. You don't want any of that mess mixed in with your work.

So, you should always cleanse the candle before you burn it.

When I buy a candle in the store I always blow my breath over it before I put it in the basket. This helps a little. Once I get it home, I either run it under some cool running water or wipe it down with some type of water or wash. There are a couple of ways I cleanse my candles. I will run them under cool running water if I am not going to be working with them right away. I will make a wash of saltwater and wipe them off, or I will add a capful of vinegar to a bowl of water and use that wash to clean them. This way you get a clean candle, and the only thing it will be filled with is your prayers and petitions.

I had an elder who kept his candles in rock salt until he was ready to burn them. He believed that the wax of a candle is like a magnet and will pull feelings and such into it. Of course, back in the seventies most workers made their own candles. He really believed that any upset in the home where the candles were stored would affect the candle, and therefore the burn. I must say I think he was on the right track about the wax being like a magnet. My nana used to stand hers up in salt for twenty-four hours before she worked with them. You can cleanse them any way you want to, but they definitely need to be cleansed before you work with them. Once you get them clean, you can store them until you need them.

CANDLE COLORS

For candle work, you can do some type of divination to see what color you may need. For example, I work with blue candles for prosperity and they really work well; this I found working with my pendulum. Here are some other suggestions for which colors to use to achieve certain results:

- Red: Red promotes love. It is worked with to represent the blood, to heat things up, and for hot foot.
- Yellow: Bright yellow represents success, the sun, and prosperity.
- Green: Green represents money and nature growing in its fullest. Work with this color when you are trying to draw in total success.
- Blue: Blue draws in not only prosperity but also peace. It is worked with a lot for a peaceful home and peaceful surroundings.
- Purple: Purple promotes self-power. It is also used when working with Saint Martha.

- White: White signifies holiness and purity and can be used as a blank slate for a variety of uses. It also can symbolize you, the person you're reading for, or the ancestors.
- Black: Black absorbs. Use it in reversals or unblockings to suck up bad energy.
- Rainbow: This covers everything: love, reversal, power, prosperity, and more.

BRINGING THAT CANDLE TO LIFE

A candle is just a stick of wax until you add life to it. The only time you would not pray over a candle is when the candle is being worked with for reversal or cleansing works. This is because you don't want to fill the candle with a bunch of products and prayer, because then it would be too full to pull a crossed condition or jinx off of you. I was taught that a reversal candle was to simply be spiritually cleansed before working with it, but it should never be loaded with product. The same thing with a cleansing candle; you simply need to clean the candle to remove whatever it picked up in the store.

You can't just set a light to a candle and expect it to do a successful job for you because not much is going to happen. That candle has to be worked in order for it to do the job you need it to do.

Most of the time, the first thing I do is mark my candles up with the name of the target. I have a nail I always work with. (Note: you should only work with a blade if you are trying to cut something away. I know some folks from other traditions mark their candles with a blade, but in my world blades cut magic!) Once I have the candle marked, I hold it up to my mouth and blow three breaths onto it; I do this three times. Then I pray my prayer and petition three times. After that, I lightly oil the candle and then I roll it either in some type of powder or I roll it in a mixture of roots and herbs. The ingredients used in the powder and oil depend on what type of job I am doing.

Then it depends on what type of job I am doing as to what I do next; I will either light the candle right away, or I will wrap it up to burn at a later time. Once you have the candle dressed and blessed, it is ready to work with.

It is important that, as the candle burns, you go back and forth at least three times during the burning and say your prayer and petition over it. You also need to have a glass of cool water sitting on your altar next to the candle so it can help draw spirit in. There is a lot more work in a successful job than most want to do, but if you want to be a good worker you have to put the time in. Nothing is free—ever!

READING THE BURN

If you have ever watched the flame of a candle, then you know that each one burns differently. No two candles will ever burn the same. I feel that each candle has its own spirit. I have been making my own candles since the days when gulf wax was the only candle wax you could find unless you owned a candle-making company. Traditionally, candles were made with paraffin wax and cotton twine. Nowadays you can get many different types of wax to make candles with. I think very few folks make candles out of straight paraffin wax today.

Most of the candles made today are made with beeswax, soy wax, or a mixture of paraffin wax and either beeswax or soy wax. The ingredients and the wick make a difference in how the candle burns. You also have to take into account the candle maker's mood, and whether they are a spiritual worker or not. I have always believed that the wax is like a magnet and holds the prayers and petitions that are prayed into it while the candle is made. I think that this is why candle magic is so powerful. Not only does the wax hold the memory of the prayer and the petition prayed into it, but the flame draws spirit.

Sometimes the flame of a candle tells the story by its actions. I feel that spirit speaks through the wax and the flame of a candle. You may be thinking, *What in the world is she talking about?* Let me explain. When you are burning candles and the candle has burned out, you may see a shape in the wax. This could be a shape that looks like a snake or a bird; both of these animals bring messages of wisdom. Another thing that could happen is the flame could give off a lot of smoke, or it might make a lot of crackling sounds; these things also tell us something about the candle burn.

Candles are burned to bring forth some type of action, be it positive or negative. It all depends on the reason the candle is being burned. I like to throw out a little caution and say that every action causes a reaction and we alone are responsible for the works we do. If you are working with a candle, I think it's important that you watch it as it burns to know of any sounds or any changes in the flame. These things will give you a message on the outcome of the burn or possibly some information you need to know about the work.

Don't overthink this; just relax, watch, and listen to how the candle acts. Each of us has our own way of seeing things, so there is truly no right or wrong way to read a candle as it burns. I am simply sharing information that may be helpful to some of you. Following, you will find a list of a few of the actions the flame might have.

Flame Patterns

Double Wick Flame

In my world, a double-wick flame is the luckiest flame you can get when you are doing candle divination! It is a blessing. The double flame is a promise from spirit that your burn will be a total success! The double flame usually happens when the wick of the candle burns into two pieces and the flame keeps burning. This is truly a gift from spirit. It is especially powerful in burns concerning reversal work.

Small, Steady Flame

A small, steady flame shows that spirit is there working on your petition. There could be issues going on behind the scene that you are unaware of. This is not a bad burn, just a slow one. I would do some blockbusting if this candle was for healing, money, or success.

Blue Flame

A blue flame is a blessing coming your way (or at least that is what I was taught). The blue is spirit sitting on your candle.

Wick Will Not Stay Lit

If you try to light a candle and the wick will not light or will not stay lit, there could be two reasons. The first is a mundane reason: the wick just isn't any good or it was not coated with wax before it was put in the candle. The wick is the head of the candle and the wax is the body; if the head don't work, the body ain't gonna work.

Now for the spiritual reason: It could be that whatever you are trying to do is not needed or there could be some type of block. This is why it is important to do a divination before you decide to do any type of work. Divination is a large part of everything we do within this work. If you don't know for sure what you need, then you are spinning your wheels trying to do a job that shouldn't be done.

Flame Goes Out

If you light a candle and the flame keeps going out, I would first check the wick. If the wick isn't being flooded by wax, then I would do a divination to see what in the world is going on. There are times when you get a candle that just will not burn, because the wick is no good, but these are far and few between. If the candle will not stay lit, then I would say either you have some serious blocks or spirit doesn't want you doing that job. I was taught that if the flame of the candle goes out, either someone is working against the work or there are blocks in the way from the work being a success. If this happens, you should do a spiritual cleansing and then restart the burn.

Big Flame

If you have a big flame on your candle and you trimmed the wick before you lit it, I would have to say spirit is working overtime for you. When this happens, the candle usually burns out fast; this is good and not so good. If the candle burns out too fast, it doesn't have time to do it's job, but the good thing is you know spirit is listening to your prayers. Before that candle burns completely out, you should light another one and continue your work.

Active Flame

I was taught that if a flame moves a lot and gets really big, that is spirit doing the work for you. For me this is a very good sign.

Relighting Flame

Science will tell you that if you try to put a candle out by snuffing it out and it lights back up, air got to the wick before the fire went completely out. That's what science will say. What I was taught is that if a candle flame relights itself, then spirit was not done with the work. If this should happen, you need to let the candle remain lit until it burns completely out.

Movement and Noise

As a young worker I was taught that if a candle has a lot of movement and noise, then it is a sign that the spirits are battling for your case. When this happens, I place the candle in a tin can with some red wine poured in the bottom. It's a trick I was taught many years ago to feed the spirit. I will also light a white candle and place it beside the tin can, so it can help the spirits of the first candle do their job. I was taught if a candle makes crackling sounds that it is spirit praying in your defense. If this happens know that spirit is there with you.

Smoke Patterns

Soot

If you burn many candles, you will see soot sometimes. It can either be white or black. There are two reasons you might see soot on a glass or coming from a stick candle. First, the mundane reason. Once again, here we are with the wick. If the wick is saturated with oils it will smoke, or if the wick is made of the wrong type of material it may smoke. Also, if you overload your candles with oils and herbs then there is a chance that not only will they smoke but they could burst or catch fire. It's important to do some type of divination to see what exactly is going on.

Now for the spiritual reason. If the smoke is black, it could mean that there is opposition to the work, or blocks. If you see white soot on the top of a glass candle that clears up, I was taught that spirit moved something out of the way. They cleared something. If you get white soot on your candle I would do a good brush down and say some prayers for the blocks to be removed. After the candle burns out, I would do another candle for the same job and compare that with the first burn. Sometimes things are going on with us and we don't even realize anything is really wrong until we burn that candle and it gets all sooty and gets our attention.

If you are burning a candle and you notice soot and black smoke and you have not overloaded it with herbs and oils, then you may have an issue. I don't put my candles out when they smoke—I let them burn completely out—but I will do spiritual cleansings as they are burning. If you are sure that you have not overloaded the candle and it is giving off black smoke, then you need to pull out your divination tool and see what is going on. Once you see what the issue is, then you will be able to fix whatever is going on. I would still do at least a set of three cleansing baths and then move on with whatever else I think I need to do.

If the black smoke is just partway on the glass and then clears up toward the bottom of the glass as it burns, I would say that the candle removed something that shouldn't have been there, and spirit got out of the way and the candle started burning clear again. It is important that you do divination on any type of smoky burn. Something is going on, and divination is truly the only way to find out what it is. I would once again keep notes on any burn that I did that had soot on it.

Smoke Follows You

The ole folks say that "smoke follows beauty," but when you are doing candle divination this is not always true. If the smoke of a candle that you are burning for success, prosperity, a job, or love comes to you, then it is said that it will be a successful burn. So, any burn you are doing to draw something good into your life will be a success. But (there is always that but!) if you are doing works to cross folks up, promote domination, or perpetuate a hotfoot situation, you might want to do a divination because this could be a sign that the work was unjustified, and you may feel a taste of your own medicine! This is why divination before any type of work is a must.

Smoke Goes Away from You

If your candle is smoking and the smoke is moving away, this could mean that the work is not going well and there may be some blocks going on with the work. This is the time for divination. You need to see what else can be done to get the work moving in the right direction, especially if the work is being done for reversal, crossing, or moving someone or something out of the way. If the candle is being done for healing or cleansing, I would say that the candle burn is a success as the smoke is moving away from you.

Other Burn Patterns

Hole in the Candle

There are times when a candle will burn only in the center. This could be caused because the wrong size wick was used when the candle was made, or the candle should have had two wicks. Or it could be that there are blocks going on, and the walls in the candle represent that. This would be a good time to do a divination and also do a quick cleansing. I would let the candle continue to burn, but right before it burns out I would start another one and place them side by side.

Candle Busts

As a young worker, I was taught that if a candle burst then it either took a hit for you or it removed a block out of your way. You may be asking, what does took a hit mean? In my world, it means that someone is trying to work on you and the work hit the candle instead. Some folks will say spirit stopped the work because it was unjustified, or they didn't approve of the work being done. This is one time where if you have never done a divination on your candle work that you truly need too. If the work was stopped by spirit, then you surely want to know so you can find out another way to proceed. If the candle removed something from you or if it took a hit for you, it is also important to find out through divination what is going on. If you are going to do the work then you need to stay on top of it to make sure you are not just spinning your wheels doing work that will not come to light.

Fast-Burning Candle

I was always taught that if a candle burns really fast that you need to light another one. Spirit is working fast for your cause, but another candle should be lit when the first one goes out.

Slow-Burning Candle

If a candle burns really slowly, either the wick is no good or someone is battling against you. If this happens, you need to do more in order to succeed.

Wax Patterns

Wax Runs

If your wax runs as the candle burns, then you need to pay attention as to how it's running. Does the wax run away from the candle or does it pool around the candle? If the wax pools around the candle, then it is important to do a reading on the burn because there may be something there blocking the work. Remember, a circle is a never-ending thing and nothing can get in or out.

Then we have the wax that flows away from the candle. I was taught that this is a sign something is being taken away from you unless the candle is being burned for love or attraction work. If the candle is being burned for love or attraction, then I'd do a reading because there could be something in the way of success of the burn.

Wax Doesn't Run

If a candle is made out of solid beeswax, then there should be no runs in the wax. If the right size wick is used to make the candle, then there will be no runs. Just throwing that out there.

If your candle burns without any runs, then that is a great sign! It means that spirit heard your prayer and petition and they will be answering it.

The one thing that you really need to do is pay attention to how your burn is going and do your divination to find out what is really going on. Divination is a must in any kind of spiritual work; it can save you a lot of wasted time and money. The spirits that walk with you will always guide you in the direction you should be going in; you simply have to listen.

SIGNS IN THE WAX

Sometimes when we burn a candle there is leftover wax. This wax sometimes takes on different shapes. Below, you will find some different shapes and how to discern them. I was taught to burn stick candles for work. I like working with them because you can mark them up and roll them in an herbal mixture. They also leave good information when the candle has burned out. You can look at the wax that is left and see if there is an extra message for you there. Sometimes you will see shapes of things you recognize and other times it may just be melted wax on a plate.

I was taught that if there is an *unbroken* ring of wax in the bottom of a glass candle, then there are blocks in the way and cleansing must be done in order to remove them. If there is a *broken* ring of wax on the bottom, blocks will be moved out of the way but there is still work that needs to be done. When this happens, I'll do a quick brush down or cleansing and then light another candle.

There may be times when you deliberately burn a stick candle to see what signs might be there. When I was a young worker trying to learn about candle readings, one of my mentors had me deliberately drip wax from a candle that was worked to find out what message spirit had for me. This is how you do it.

Simple Stick Candle Practice

Get a candle of the appropriate color (see earlier section on color meanings). Wearing gloves, wipe the candle off with a rag dipped in a little ammonia, (make sure you wear gloves because ammonia is strong) and wait for the ammonia to dry completely. Then clean the ammonia off the candle with some olive oil. Once you have the candle cleansed and dressed, hold the candle up to your mouth and blow three breaths on it and tell spirit what you're looking for. Repeat the breaths and your petition three times.

Light the stick candle. Holding the candle, look at the flame for a minute then tilt the candle a little so the wax falls onto a heat-resistant plate. Don't worry about how the wax is shaping up; just focus on your petition and what you are trying to find out. Once about twenty drops of wax have fallen onto the plate, put the candle out. If you don't find what you are looking for, you can repeat the work. This is an easy way to do candle divination if you need information in a hurry. The trick is not to focus on what the wax is doing! Let spirit speak through the wax; you simply let the wax fall wherever it will.

Below you will find a list of things you might see in a puddle of wax after your candle has burned out. This is not an exact science, as it is spiritual, and you will be using your gifts to see what is there.

Baby: The birth of something new, be it a business, a new baby, or a new love affair.

Balloon: Whatever the issue is, it won't last long, like a balloon with the air let out of it.

Beans: Prosperity is on its way, or money difficulties will be over soon.

Bed: Depends on if the bed is made or not: a made bed represents a happy, peaceful home; and an unmade bed represents a home in turmoil.

Bells: A warning that something or someone is coming; or to call someone or something.

Bird: Birds bring messages. They mean different things to different people. If you ask my daughter about hearing a hoot owl, she will tell you it's calling for death; if you ask me, I'd say that the hoot owl is wise and with it comes wisdom. My daughter got her belief in the hoot owl from my mama; so did I, but I learned divination is the key to figuring out what is really going on.

Boo Hag: If your wax is shaped like the ole boo hag, you definitely need to do some strong cleansing work and divination to find out what exactly is going on. In the South, the boo hag comes to you in your sleep and can suck your breath away. It is also believed that she can be sent to torment the target. The ole folks say she has red eyes, steel gray hair, and a face that will torment you if you wake up.

Bridge: Bridges usually go over water; water cleanses. If you see a bridge, it could mean a cleansing is needed or you are being cleansed of something.

Broom: Brooms are for cleansing and protection, so I would suggest doing some cleansing and protection work.

Cat: Something is hidden or someone is being sly.

Chain: Something is locked down or bound; divination is needed to see exactly what is going on.

Circle: A never-ending bond, be it good or bad.

Cloud: Something is moving away from you, or a threat is moving toward you.

Cross: A crossroads; change is coming. It is up to you to decide what that change will be. Do a strong divination to make sure you pick the right road. There will be no stopping this change, so make the best of it.

Crown: Success in all you do.

Cup: It depends if the cup is full or empty: If the cup is full and you have been having issues, they will be resolved. If the cup is empty, then you need to dig deeper and see what is going on.

Dog: Folks are very loyal to you. However, if the dog is not the full shape, you have folks around you who are not loyal.

Egg: The birth of something new—a job, a bundle of joy, or something you have been trying to get off the ground.

Fan: Things are about to be stirred up.

Feather: A message is coming, or spirit has a gift for you.

Fish: Look out—something good is coming your way.

Grass: Feed your needs so they will grow and prosper.

Heart: Love and happiness—unless the heart is cracked, which means heartache is coming.

House: Family, happiness, and love. Peace will reign—unless the house is cracked. In that case, do some type of peaceful home work to ensure that peace reigns on the home and family.

Key: A key pointed upward opens doors; a key pointed downward closes doors. If the key is whole, new opportunities will be opening up; but if the key not whole then I would suggest doing some cleansing and road opening work.

Ladder: Climbing upward or downward, especially with employment and relationships. An unbroken ladder means things are moving upward (a raise or a promotion at work). A broken ladder speaks of breakups and job changes.

Leaf/Leaves: Growth; things going well. If the leaf is half formed or broken, there are issues that need to be looked at. I would definitely do some divination on the situation.

Lion: You're king of the jungle. Be patient and look at the whole situation. If the lion is cracked, watch out for an attack; keep your protections up and be watchful.

Moon: A change is coming.

Pen: Expect a letter or an important paper.

Pipe: Peace; or a message is coming your way.

Ring: A marriage; or something that is never ending.

Safety Pin: Used for nailing down or protection. An open safety pin indicates you are well protected. A closed one means you have some blocks and need to do some cleansing and divination.

Scissors: Cut unwanted blocks and issues away. Divination might reveal what needs to be cut and cleared.

Shoe: In "foot track" Conjure, a work is laid down for the target to walk into—they have no clue that they have been conjured. Then they track the work throughout their lives. If your candle's wax is a shoe, look into it through divination. If the shoe has flaws, something was broken away from you.

Snake: Wisdom, and a heads up that maybe something shady is going on.

Spider Web: Look out for traps being set for you.

Stick: Commune more with your ancestors and the spirits that walk with you.

Sun: If the sun is whole, lots of good things are coming your way—warmth, sunshine, prosperity—but if the sun is misshapen you need to look into it. Too much sun can destroy.

Tongue: A well-formed tongue means folks are speaking well of you; a half-formed or cracked tongue means folks are spreading lies and vicious rumors about you. Do some divination, and then some strong cleansing and protection work.

Tree: You have a strong foundation and things will continue to get even better. If the tree is misshapen, some divination and cleansing work is needed to build up that foundation.

Umbrella: A whole umbrella means you are well shielded from life's problems; a broken one means you need to reinforce your protections.

Wheel: Things are going to start moving forward. If it is a broken wheel, you are in a rut and need to do some divination to see how to get yourself moving again.

Witch: Something mysterious is going on—something hidden. Use divination to find out what you are not seeing.

Worm: Many worms eat away at plants and sometimes even animals. I would do some serious reversal work and then look deep to see what is really going on.

A WORK TO SEE WHAT'S HIDDEN

As I am finishing up the book, I thought of a trick for revealing hidden things that I haven't worked with in a long time. I've not ever heard of anyone writing about it or sharing it, so this may be the first time it has gotten out.

You will need:

- 5 stick candles
- A glass of blue water

You need to do a cleansing first—this can be either a simple brush down or a cleansing bath. Then set up your ancestor altar.

Mark an eye on each of the candles, then pray over four of the five candles and petition your ancestors to show you what you need to see.

Place the blue water on the altar, then place the four candles around the water in this order: top, bottom, right, left. You are trying to communicate with spirit and your ancestors, so you want the roads open for discernment.

Light each of the candles in the order you set them down and pray Luke 8:17 over each one as you light it:

> *"For nothing is secret that will not be revealed, nor anything hidden that will not be known and come to light."*

Lastly, light the fifth candle and petition your ancestors to show you what is hidden. Then tilt the candle over the blue water and let one drop of wax fall while you pray Luke 8:17. Then let another drop of wax fall in the water while you say the prayer again. Repeat this process three times, then put the candle you are holding out. Sit in front of your altar as the other candles burn and look into the water. Just relax and don't try too hard.

See what shapes the wax has made. Write down whatever you see. This is a simple but effective work to see what is hidden. It really doesn't take a lot of work; you have to remember the ancestors didn't have a lot to work with, but they were clever and held the power of the ancestors in their hands.

ANOTHER WORK TO SEE WHAT'S HIDDEN

There are times when things are hidden from us that we just cannot see. Sometimes there are things going on in the background that we have no clue who or what the cause is. I often work with my ancestors because they always have my best interest at heart.

The ancestors watch out for us when we don't even realize that they are there. What some folks don't understand is that you are never really alone; your ancestors are always there. They may not interfere in your daily life, but they do watch and listen—and like all spirits they see everything that is done, whether it be in the dark or the light. I have learned that not all folks have your best interest at heart. At times we trust folks that we shouldn't, and things go on that we know nothing about.

I wanted to share this work because I think that it will be helpful for folks who can't quite find out what is really going on behind the scenes. Nothing is free in this life, so in order to get information you have to do the work. I wrote the following prayer calling on my ancestors because my ancestors walked so strong with me. I can't ever remember a time that they were not there. If you don't work with your ancestors, then I would suggest that before you do this work you set up an altar to them and you get to know them. It can be just a simple table with a glass of water and a candle on it. Your ancestors are there to help you find your way and to better your life. You simply have to open the door and let them in.

This works really well when things are hidden and you've tried and tried to get to the bottom of the situation; your ancestors will show you exactly what is going on. You simply have to do the work.

You will need:

- 5 white stick candles
- A nail
- White handkerchief

This work takes five days to complete, but some folks may be blessed to see what they're looking for after the first burn.

To start, take a nail and write on the candles what you are looking for. I use what I call "power words" which represent what my petition is trying to achieve. You could write words or phrases like "gossip," "truth," "what is hidden," or "show me the truth." It really all depends on what you are trying to find out.

Once you have your candle marked up, hold it up to your mouth and say your prayer over it. Then light the candle and pay attention to how the flame moves. Say your prayer and petition over the candle at least three times as the candle burns. Let the candle burn completely out. If there is any leftover wax, notice what kind of shapes it has and then set it aside. Once you've said your ending prayers of thanks to your ancestors, place the leftover wax in a white handkerchief and tie a loose knot in the top.

Place the handkerchief under your pillow when you go to bed that night. Repeat the process until you have burned all five of your candles and all five pieces of leftover wax are tied in your handkerchief. Keep the handkerchief under your pillow until you get the answers you are looking for. Once you have your answers, you can bury the wax in a nice pot with ivy in it, or bury it under a tree. Since you are trying to draw information to yourself, I would do this work when the hands of the clock are going upward.

Ancestor Prayer

I call on my ancestors known and unknown and ask that you show me what is hidden from my sight________ (name what you are looking for). I ask that you show me whatever traps or obstacles have been set in my way. Bring what is done in the dark into the light. Gracious ancestor who walks with me day and night, draw forth what is hidden into plain sight!

No one should fear their ancestors, but I know some folks are not used to working with them or honoring them. They really should be at the top of your prayer line, but we are all raised differently. That is why I've added Bible verses here as an alternative. Follow the same instructions as above, but simple pray one of these verses instead of the ancestor prayer.

> *He reveals deep and hidden things; he knows what is in the darkness, and the light dwells with him.*
>
> (DANIEL 2:22)

> *The secret things belong to the Lord our God, but the things that are revealed belong to us and to our children forever, that we may do all the words of this law.*
>
> (DEUTERONOMY 29:29)

> *But there is nothing covered up that will not be revealed and hidden that will not be known. Accordingly, whatever you have said in the dark will be heard in the light,*

and what you have whispered in the inner rooms will be proclaimed upon the housetops.

(LUKE 12:2–3)

For nothing is secret that will not be revealed, nor anything hidden that will not be known and come to light.

(LUKE 8:17)

CANDLE AND APPLE DIVINATION

Not long ago, I found out someone tried to trick my truck—there was some red wax by the windshield wipers. I told my friend Tessa about it, and she suggested doing this working with apples. I'd done a similar work many times before with a potato, but this was my first time doing the job with apples. Trust and believe, I check my truck now every time I get in it. I'm almost positive that someone in the city laid that trick, because I've lived in the same place for thirty years and everyone knows not to mess around my home.

I believe what was placed right below my windshield wiper was a soft wax Conjure ball or a soft wax Conjure doll. The color red is worked with to represent the blood, to heat things up, for hot foot, and for love. I don't believe anyone was trying to work a love trick on me; I do, however, believe that someone was either trying to hotfoot me out of the city or cause issues for me. I don't know how long that wax had been there, but it had been there for a good minute, so whoever laid the trick basically wasted their time and mine. But the one good thing is I now know for a fact that someone is working against me.

Let me explain how the apples work. Like I said, I'd never done this work with apples; I'd always used potatoes. I learned a long time ago that if you want to find out who is working against you or who is hiding in the shadows plantin' seeds, you can do it by writing their name on a potato, putting their photo inside the potato, and then seeing which potato starts to rot first. I think apples will show a sign even faster than potatoes.

In the old days, potatoes were used for many different types of work—crossing work, healing work—it just depended on the work and where the potato was placed. This time, I'm working with Saint Martha the Dominator. I have worked with her for more years than I've lived in this house. I trust her, and I know she will get to the bottom of this.

This is how I was taught to do this work. The only thing I have changed is that I'm working with apples instead of potatoes. This trick can be worked to really find out all kinds of information. For this one, though, we are going to see exactly who planted that trick on my truck.

To start, I place five red apples in a circle. In the center I place the wax from my truck that I dug off with a knife. This way Saint Martha will have a link with whoever planted that trick. I place a purple candle in the center of the apples on top of the wax to feed Saint Martha as she works. I believe that it's someone with not much experience, because they would know not to ever plant a trick that could be found. What they were not thinking of—and this once again shows inexperience—is that wax holds a memory. It also holds pieces of their DNA, and this is part of their spirit. If you are going to do this kind of work, you need to always think about your actions and remember that every action causes a reaction.

Around the apples I have placed four black candles in the shape of a cross. These are not for crossing or for cursing; they are there to pull off any of the ruminants of the work that may be left in the wax. You know, I'm more amused than I am upset. This was such an amateur trick that it's laughable, but this work will show me exactly who did it if I write the right names on the apples.

Sometimes it takes a minute to do a job if you're going to do it right. Yes, I have my suspicions of who could have placed that trick on my truck, but I'm a seasoned worker and so I know that I need to do a divination on the names first before I go writing any names on any apples. I'll do this working with a pendulum board.

Clean a space for you to do the work. If you already have a space, then work on that space. I didn't do this work with my ancestors, because I felt they would go too far getting me justice. Since no harm was really done, I simply wanted to know who did the work and then left it with Saint Martha for her to deal with. Sometimes less is more.

Take the names of the targets (these are the folks that divination showed you could possibly be at fault) and carve one name into each apple. I used a blade to do this. Once you have the names on the apples, you can go to your ancestors or to someone else that you work with and petition them to show you who is working against you. The apple that starts to rot first is the one who is working against you. Once you find out this information, you and you alone are responsible for the actions you take. I am a justified worker, so I always let spirit dish out the punishment because I know the target will get their just reward—no more, no less.

I started with five apples. Out of those five, three turned bad at the same time. I know that justice has been served on two of them, but I haven't heard anything about the third one yet. It was fast work on Saint Martha's part! Less than three weeks! Folks really need to remember that every action causes a reaction, and unjustified works will always backfire on you if the target knows what they are doing. Be mindful of your actions, and remember: you can't hide from a person's ancestors or the spirits that walk with them.

OCHOSSI

I was doing a reversal on myself and my businesses, working with a rainbow candle. I decided to burn the rainbow candle because it covers everything: love, reversal, power, prosperity, and more. This was the first time I burned a seven-colored candle as a reversal. I must say, I was a little shocked when I saw a wall of wax just sitting there and a perfect bow and arrow formed by the burnt off pieces of wick. I am just a plain ole Conjure woman, but I have seen information shared by folks and I knew that the shape of the bow and arrow was just like the one of Ochossi, a warrior spirit. I was thinking to myself, *What in the world is going on with this burn? And why is Ochossi's bow and arrow there along with mermaids?*

You never know what message the ancestors and spirit are going to send your way. That is why being able to hear them and to understand what they are trying to tell you is so important. You should always honor your ancestors and keep an open line of communication with them. They are your first line of defense and your protectors! Keep them fed and uplifted!

First, I do not practice Santeria; and second, I do not mess with things I know very little or almost nothing about. I don't trust just anybody to give me information on what I don't know, either, but I knew I had to find out the answer to this burn. I felt I knew what it meant, but I needed someone in the religion to answer my questions. One, it could mean that Ochossi was coming to help me with the reversal; or two, someone had sent him after me and it was unjust, so he showed himself to me. I figured someone had sent him after me, but I needed that second opinion.

I battled with myself for a good thirty minutes. *Do I really want someone knowing my business? Do I really need a second opinion ego talking? Should I just leave it alone and let it go?* Every answer I came up with was, "No, no, no. Call someone for help." I broke down and called Candelo Kimbisa, another worker who is a Santero. I trust him, and I knew he wouldn't feed me a bunch of BS. Sure enough, he said almost the same thing I thought. Someone must have sent Ochossi to attack me, but for whatever reason Ochossi showed himself to me. I'm very thankful that he showed himself to me, because from what I know of him, Ochossi shoots straight and is all about justice—which is probably why he didn't hit me. Because I haven't done anything to anyone, so the hit would have been unjustified.

You can do the work, but in the end, spirit has control over how the work turns out. I am so glad this reversal work showed what was going on and what could happen. It's important to remember that once a job is done it is out of the worker's hands and it is up to spirit what will happen next. As you can see with this reversal, the truth came out by spirit's own hand. Folks are going to learn that you cannot command spirit! In the end, the spirit is in full control—and if you think you can command spirit, then you need to get your ego in check because you are fooling yourself! I'm sure there will be some who read this and think that I don't know what I am talking about. All I can say is, keep fooling yourself.

All a worker can do is practice the work. Once you petition spirit or the ancestors to step in, that work is no longer in your control. Period. The end! You really should make sure that the work you are doing is justified—or, like this reversal, spirit may decide to go with the target and then you would have done all that work for nothing. If you don't like someone or if they have just made you mad, walk away and petition your ancestors to right the wrong, that is really all you ever have to do anyway. The ancestors will always take care of the rest. Don't let your ego get you into trouble.

DIVINATION THROUGH EGGS

Who would have thought that an egg could do more than feed us? When many folks see eggs, they think of breakfast. When I see eggs, I think of all the wonderful things they can do when you work with them. I first learned how to work with eggs when I was seventeen years old. I was a young mother at seventeen, and my baby boy had asthma. It seemed like we were at the hospital every other week. When he would have an asthma attack, that would cause him to run a fever and have difficulty breathing. He had asthma medicine and a breathing machine to help him breathe. His *madrina's* (godmother) daddy, who we call the old *padrino* (godfather), was a healer. He taught me how to help my baby by working with eggs, herbs, and candles.

Eggs are a wonderful tool because they are a living thing and can actually hatch into a living thing. So they seem to work well for clearing off crossed conditions, blocking nightmares, and doing anything else that can be pulled from the body spiritually. I work with fresh eggs, but I am lucky and have chickens. I have found that store-bought eggs usually have a watery white, which might not give a good reading. Watery whites come from the chicken being given too much water—or at least that is what my mama used to say. If you can't get fresh eggs, then try to get eggs from the farmers market if you have one near you. Nowadays, in small towns there is usually someone selling fresh eggs. If you can't get fresh ones, then just work with what you've got.

Egg cleansing has become popular since I learned how to do it in the seventies. It seems like everyone now is spiritual cleansing with eggs. I continue to work with the same technique that the old padrino taught me many years ago. It has never let me down.

BASIC EGG CLEANSING

You need to do a cleansing bath or brush down before and after if you are doing an egg cleansing on someone other than yourself. Of course, if you are doing a brush down with an egg on yourself, then you should follow it up with a cleansing bath and some prayer work, depending on how the egg turns out after it is dropped in the glass.

You will need:

- A glass of cool water
- A pinch of salt that you have prayed Psalm 23 over.
- 1 egg at room temperature
- 1 white stick candle that you have prayed over[1]
- 2 broom straws[2]

If you are doing a cleansing on yourself, you can touch the egg. If you are doing a cleansing on someone else, then please have a couple of inches between the person's body and the egg. Starting at the crown of the head, hold the egg in your dominant hand and go downward and outward. Repeat this process a few times, then move over the rest of the head area, always going downward and never moving in a

[1] Note: I don't tell folks how to pray or what to pray—that is personal—but for this white candle you need to pray that its light will help clear away anything that is there and that the light of the candle guide the condition into the egg.

[2] I was taught to take the straw right out of the broom you sweep with. Please don't work with a plastic broom for this. I know y'all are thinking no one would ever do that, but I have been asked in the past if that is okay and the answer is no, it isn't.

back-and-forth motion. As a young worker, I was told that moving in a back-and-forth motion confuses spirit and just stirs up the mess. The egg may become warm in your hand, or it might feel heavy.

Once you feel the change in the egg, crack it into the water. Take the shell and offer it to a tree or throw it in the crossroads—either way will work. Next, place the broom straw on top of the water in the shape of a cross. This is done to nail the condition down in the water. Light your candle and place it behind the glass so the flame shines into the water. (Sometimes I will light the candle before I drop the egg into the water it all depends on how spirit leads me.)

For the next twenty-four hours, keep an eye on the egg to see if there are any signs about the condition that was removed. You will see many different things in the glass when you drop the egg in the water. It may be a bunch of bubbles. It could be streams of white all the way down to the bottom. I remember one time my son's fever was so high that when I dropped the egg in the water it truly looked like the white had been cooked. The egg had pulled so much fever out of his little body that it cooked once it dropped into the water.

After the twenty-four hours have passed, dispose of the egg, making sure you don't get any of the water on you. There are a few ways you can dispose of it: 1) you can flush it down the toilet (this is the preferred method for some workers); 2) you can dump it in the crossroads (make sure it isn't one you travel often); 3) you can give it to a tree; or 4) you can dump it in the graveyard. I personally do not advise this last method unless you are a seasoned worker. Here's why: If you are doing a set of egg cleansings, then your spirit will be opened and fresh. I really don't think you should go traipsing through graves with a fresh spirit like that. You just might pick up more than the condition you took off. Please use common sense!

Divination by eggs is a gift; it truly comes from the spirits that walk with you sharing their knowledge to help you understand. I'm sure some of you might be wondering what in the world made me decide to add egg divination to this book. Well, there are two reasons. One, I think that everyone should know how to cleanse with eggs. And two, I wanted to share my last egg cleansing with y'all. The egg had a blood spot in it. Seasoned workers know that before you work with an egg you should always hold it up to a candle flame to make sure there isn't anything in it. I did this, and I still got a blood spot.

So, what happens if you get a blood spot in an egg cleansing? And what exactly does that mean? I was taught that if there is a blood spot in the egg, then it is a sign of witchcraft—the dark arts. This is considered a curse! When this happens, you need to go to your ancestors so they can remove the curse and put it right back on the source it came from. Then you should follow through with at least five more egg cleansings, offering each one to your ancestors.

Before we move on to how to read what you see in the glass of water, I wanted to share one more way to do an egg cleansing.

SIMPLE EGG CLEANSING

Put an egg in a brown paper bag and place it under your bed where your head lays on your pillow at night. Different workers will say leave it there a number of days; the numbers will vary between workers. I was taught to do an egg every three days for the Holy Trinity. After three days, crack the egg into a glass of water. Place a fresh egg in the bag and put it back under your bed. You will do a total of three eggs in nine days. By the time you have finished the last egg, you should be feeling better and sleeping much more peacefully.

HOW TO READ AN EGG

I'm sure there are many interpretations of how to read an egg; it's all in the perception of the worker and how close they walk with their spirits. Here are just a few to give you an idea of what you are looking for.

Blood in the egg: a crossed condition caused by witchcraft.

Lots of bubbles: the condition is being lifted off of you and brought to the top.

Eye in the egg: be it for love or evil, you have someone watching you.

A wall of white: this can be one of two things: an enemy is trying to block you, or your spirits are protecting you. Do further divination.

Water is clear: this is a great sign you are spiritually clean.

Egg smells rotten: this is serious, and you must do some strong cut and clear work along with some powerful cleansing and protection work. Do more divination to find out what is really going on.

Egg smells like sulfur: this is a sign that the devil has been sent after you—or the egg could just be rotten.

I could share my interpretations with you all day long, but you may see something completely different when you are doing the work. Like any divination skill, you have to be able to discern what spirit is telling you—or in the case of reading an egg, showing you. All forms of divination should start with the ancestors, for they see all and know all. Make sure you keep your cleansings and protections up if you are going to be working for other folks. If you don't, you may be jumping out of the frying pan and into the fire and end up with more mess on you than you took off of them. Cleansing of any kind is not a game or some easy work that you just do. Remember, protection first!

EGG CLEANSING Q&A

Q: Can the egg be cold when I start my work?

A: No. The egg should be at room temperature. If it isn't, then it will be colder than the tap water you will drop it into, and that would give a false reading.

Q: Can anyone do an egg cleansing?

A: Yes and no. When you do any type of cleansing work, you should know what you are doing or you could pull the condition from the client onto yourself. If you are doing the cleansing on yourself, then you need to know how to protect yourself.

Q: Are egg cleansings safe?

A: They are as long as you respect the work and don't just go running willy-nilly doing whatever. Once you have finished the brush down, you have to be careful not to get any of the egg or water on you when you crack the egg in the water.

Q: Is one egg cleansing enough?

A: I was taught to do cleansings in sets of threes: one a day for three consecutive days. Each day the new egg should become cleaner and clearer.

Q: Can egg cleansings help with healing?

A: Nothing can ever replace medical attention; but the egg may be able to help because it draws like a magnet.

BIBLIOMANCY

Back in the day all families had a Bible, I believe, and they were called family Bibles. This is where all important events in the family were written: marriages, births, baptisms, deaths. It was a record book of the family. My birth is the last grandchild that my grandma wrote in her Bible. My granddaddy gave her the Bible on January 28, 1915, the day they were married. When she passed, my oldest sister kept it. And then when she passed, it was given to me. I keep it on my ancestor altar. Not only is it a link to my family history, but it has picked up the spirit of those who have handled it, of those who have searched out its wisdom.

Folks have been searching for help within the pages of the Bible since the beginning of the book. It isn't a new thing. Many preachers and laymen have opened that book in hopes that some light might be shown on some issue they were having. Bibliomancy, per Webster, could be the opening of any book (not just the Bible) to find an answer you may be seeking. I think that this is an art of divination that is being lost as old workers pass and the new generation of workers are not taught how it works. That is one reason I thought it was important to add it to this book of divination—so that it might live on in a book written about divination in Conjure.

Growing up, my mama was big on the Old Testament. She didn't burn candles, but she was what the ole folks call a "praying woman"; she could and would pray you into the ground if that's what it took, or she could lift you up and draw blessings upon you. It really all depended on you, I guess. We went to church every time the doors were open, but my mama didn't put up with any foolishness; the church didn't even try to tell her how to live and such. She just had that type of spirit about her; she was a no-nonsense type of woman and mother. Her own children didn't push her buttons—why in the world would a preacher try? She was fair and caring. She taught us that everyone deserved respect and honor until they didn't, no matter who they were.

Being raised Pentecostal was a blessing in its own way; you learned how to pray and what spirit feels like. I also think that all that praying helps open up your psychic abilities. They really are mystical, even though they will deny it. They also believe in prophecy. I think that the modern-day churches are throwing out all the old doctrine and the preachers are making up new ones to suit their own agendas; but for me there is no way like the old way. It is what I grew up with and what I know works very well for me.

I learned about bibliomancy around the same time I learned to do cleansing, within a year or two of each other. The way I was taught to cleanse, they go hand in hand. I didn't learn everything I know from one elder in my lifetime; there have been many. The thing is, the foundation has always been similar—only some of the steps differ. I combined them and made a whole setup for cleansings and finding out the answers to the questions needed for the cleansing.

When I am dealing with my clients or my family, divination is a must before I do anything. The first thing that is needed is to find out what is going on and if there is a way to fix the issue or if there is even an issue to be fixed. The next step is to find out how to fix it. You can find all this out by throwing the bones, laying out the cards, and, yes, opening up the Bible; it's all in the questions you ask.

I want to share with you the steps I take when a client comes to me thinking that they have a crossed condition or a block on them. You have to remember that everything that goes wrong is not a curse; sometimes things just happen. Sometimes there are lessons we need to learn, and it is not the worker's place to remove the block from the client. That is why it is so important to do a reading first; I have had spirit tell me to butt out and not do anything, and I always listen.

Like I said, the first thing I do is a reading to make sure a cleansing is needed. If I get a yes, then I set up a time for the client to come to the prayer house (where I see my clients and do my work) for the cleansing. I was taught to spread a white sheet out on the floor and to throw the bones at the client's feet just to make sure I am on the right track. Cleansing is not done lightly, and I was taught to check and recheck to make sure that is what is needed. I always pray first to make sure I am working with the right tools because no two clients are the same.

Once I have gathered all the information I can, I set up for the cleansing. I always place a candle and an egg in the sign of a cross on the floor. These are laid down top to bottom, with the egg on the inside, then left to right, because I want to lock down whatever is removed. I don't want it all over the place.

Once I have everything set up, I will have the client step into the setup. I will then give them my Bible and have them hold it between their hands while asking spirit what it is they need. You would be surprised how spot-on spirit is. It always seems to shock the client that the verse they see always pertains to what is going on in their lives. Spirit always knows what is going on and how to fix it; you simply have to know how to discern the information you are given.

Learning to listen and to act accordingly can be hard for some folks, because some can't get out of their own head long enough to understand what spirit is trying to say. You can have all the divination tools and skills in the world, but if you lack discernment you aren't going to go very far. You will be a mediocre worker, always not quite able to get the job done. Nothing is free in life, and everything begins and ends with the ancestors. They are the be-all and end-all. So, if you want to be a strong spiritual worker, then start there!

So how exactly do you do this bibliomancy stuff? If you are going to be doing cleansings and such, it is important to remember to keep yourself cleansed. When you do a cleansing on someone, you are literally pulling what is on them off. Remember, what you take off has to go somewhere; please make sure it doesn't end up on you or in your space. You should always do a cleansing before and after when doing cleansings for other folks.

BASIC BIBLIOMANCY

You will need a glass of cool water, a white stick candle, and a Bible. Make sure you are spiritually cleansed and spiritually protected. Dress the crown of your head and your hands with olive oil you have prayed Psalm 23 into.

When you are ready, light the candle and call on your ancestors. Offer them the candle and the cool glass of water. Petition them to show you what it is you need to see. Petition them to show you in a way you will be able to understand and will have total discernment in the direction you should go.

When you feel them there, hold the Bible between both hands and pray for discernment. Petition them to give you the answer you seek in a clear way that you will understand. Then open the Bible and read the first place your eyes fall. This should be your answer.

If it is not the answer you seek, it could be something else you need to know. I can tell you from experience that the ancestors got jokes sometimes, and if you are not clear in your petition they may not be clear in their answer. You have to always be clear in what you are asking for. Just be straight to the point; there is no need for long, drawn-out petitions. Your ancestors are there for you and they always will be. Just ask them!

THE PENDULUM

The pendulum is the first divination tool I was ever introduced to. The thing is, I didn't have a clue what divination was, because I was just a child. My mother worked with a reading on a string for as long as I can remember, and that is what we call it even today—mama's ring on a string. She would work with that string to tell what the gender of a baby was going to be, and as far as I know, she was never wrong. Now I have the ring on the string, and I work with it not only to find out the gender of babies but also to find out information. I too have never been wrong picking the gender of a child—even if it's twins, working with my mama's ring on the string, it has always read true. I guess it's from all the years of my mama working with it.

When my youngest son and his wife became expectant parents, I used the ring on the string to see what my new grandchildren were going to be, and yes, there's two of them. I asked if one was a boy, and the ring moved. I asked if one was a girl, and the ring moved. So, sure enough, we have a new set of twins: one boy and one girl. So my little cheeky daughter thought that she was going to fool me so I would be surprised, so she texted me (and of course they were all in on it) and she said, "Mama we got the results back. You're having two granddaughters," which would've been fine with me either way. I love my granddaughters. Those are shopping buddies for me. But I knew in my heart that that ring on a string had never let my mama down, and I knew it wasn't going to start with me. You know folks nowadays do these reveal parties and all this for the expectant mothers and fathers, so they had a reveal party and yes, they used smoke to show what the babies were going to be, and guess what mine was—pink and blue, just like I knew it was going to be.

I'm telling you this because some folks feel that working with a pendulum is just yes or no answers. That's not true; you can actually find out a whole lot of information working with a pendulum, and I want to share some of my knowledge with you.

The first thing you need to do is find a pendulum that you are comfortable with. It can be anything. You can tie a ring on a string. You can tie a knot on a string. Even a nail can be tied to a string and worked with as a pendulum. They sell many beautiful pendulums nowadays, so find one that you're drawn to or make your own.

The first thing that should be done when you get your pendulum home or when you get it made is to cleanse it because you don't know what type of energies it picked up before you bought it. So depending on what the pendulum is made out of, you can run it through cool running water and then give it to your ancestors or you can set it in salt for twenty-four hours and then run it through cool running water to cleanse it. You could also make a wash of bay leaf, salt, and baking soda and clean your pendulum off with that.

When your pendulum is spiritually cleansed, you need to dedicate it to your ancestors or a spirit that walks with you. Of course, for me the ancestors would be the way to go.

I know a lot of folks program their pendulums to go one way for yes and another way for no. To me this is just too confusing—especially if the pendulum is excited and working fast to try to give you your answer. I have always worked with mine to move for yes and stop for no, but when I saw this other way to work with it a few years ago, I tried it and discovered that it's not for me. I went right back to the way I know how to work with my pendulum, and that is move for yes and stop for no. This way there is no confusion about what the answer is; it's simple and straight to the point, which is the way I like to work.

When you are ready to test your pendulum, ask it questions that you already know the answers to. But before you do any type of divination with that pendulum, you need to do a cleansing—at least a brush down—and you need to have your protections up. That pendulum causes energy, which in turn is going to draw spirits.

Once you know that your pendulum is set to go, then you can start working with it. Start going slow at first, with yes and no questions. There is a way to find out more answers, though. I made an alphabetic board for my pendulum to be able to get more information. The idea behind the board is that you can go over each letter of the alphabet and see if that is a letter in the word that you're looking for.

For example, let's say you are looking for someone to name for whatever reason. You can go to your board and, starting with A, hold your pendulum over the letter and say, "Is this the first letter?" If the answer is no , then move next to the B and ask the question again. If the answer is yes, then write "B" down on a piece of paper. That is the first letter in the name that you are looking for. Since you have your first letter, you're going to move forward to find the second letter in the name you are looking for. So you go back to the A and you say, "Is the second letter an A?" and you move through the alphabet until you find all the letters that go with the name.

You can find out all kinds of information working with a pendulum and an alphabet board. There's nothing that can be hidden; you simply have to take the time to sit there and work through the alphabet. You can actually learn to work with your pendulum and board in order to help clients who are looking for specific information. The pendulum is more than just a tool that gives you yes and no answers; the key to working with the pendulum is to have patience and a strong connection with your ancestors and the spirits that walk with you.

When I get ready to work with my pendulum and my board, I go out into the prayer house where it is quiet and I know I will not be disturbed. First, I do a brush down with my broom and then another one with a white candle. I light the candle and give it to Saint Michael to protect me during the reading. Then I take a red candle and offer it to my ancestors and petition them to not only protect me but also gift me with the information I'm looking for. I place their candle on their altar in the prayer house. Next, I take a white candle and petition for the light of discernment and knowledge to come shining through during the reading, and that there be only light within the reading and all darkness is held at bay. Then I light the candle and set it on my reading table. So the protections and the ancestors are all gathered, ready to find out whatever information there is to find. At this time I will offer up a cool glass of water for the spirits and some type of smoke. Once this is a done I sit down and start to work.

You will be surprised at how fast time flies by when you're working with the pendulum and the board, but you can find out so much information. It's time-consuming, but it is well worth it if you are trying to help a family member or a client. You can literally find out what type of work you should be doing to help the client when you have a hard case. There is no limit to what the pendulum and the alphabet board can share with you. You are the only one who can set limitations on your readings. The best advice I can give you if you want to work with the alphabet board and the pendulum is to ask questions that you already know the answer to, and be patient and take your time. When my readings are over, I usually just leave the candles and let them burn out. I thank my ancestors and Saint Michael and the spirits that walk with me for coming and helping me and sharing their knowledge with me. Then I wrap my board up and put it away until next time.

WITCHEN' STICKS

We seem to always remember things that shock us or throw us off. One day my husband was late coming home from work—this was about six years ago, maybe a little longer. I remember this because he said something I wasn't in a million years expecting him to say when he answered his cell. I called because I was getting worried, and, as they do sometimes, he thought he had told me that he was going to be late, but he hadn't. He answered the phone and I immediately asked where he was and if he was okay. He says, "I'm witchen' these lines for my friend with my witchen' sticks!" Well that shut me up! Then I said, "What do you know about witchen' sticks?" He said, "I been using witchen' sticks to find underground lines that the machine can't pick up for years!"

I never knew my husband worked with witchen' sticks until that day. He said I knew because he told me when we first met. Well, I don't remember.

I wanted to add this section of the book in honor of my grandma, my elder brother Jack, and my husband. I first came to know of the witchen' stick when I was a young girl staying the summer with my grandma. I was probably eleven or twelve. My grandma kept hers hanging on the back porch, and, of course, like the touch-me-nots she had planted at the front door, I wasn't supposed to touch it. I can close my eyes to this day and feel the smooth wood of that witchen' stick. I don't know how long she had that stick, but it felt powerful when I held it.

Of course, I got in trouble for having it. She also told me that if the witchen' stick didn't like me, it could make me sick. If you tell a child they're going to get sick from touching something, they won't mess with it again. She also told me that it was a tool to find things the eyes couldn't see. I wish I could have asked her more questions, but you didn't question her.

I forgot all about the witchen' stick until I met Brother Jack at my auntie's house. Back in that day, folks still used water wells with pumps to get water. The well at the old place had gone almost dry, so it was time to find another source of water. Brother Jack was called the witchen' man. They say he could smell water under the ground. Once again, here I was infatuated with that witchen' stick—only this time I got to ask all the questions I wanted to.

I think back now, and I know brother Jack must have been lonely. He was in his seventies and a widower. He showed me how to use the witchen' sticks, but I wasn't allowed to touch them because I was expecting and it's a big no-no for an expecting mother to work with the witchen' sticks. Some will say that is a old wives' tale, but I wasn't testing it. My elder told me no; no means no! I did get to watch him and walk with him, though. He said the same thing my grandma and now my husband have since told me: not everyone can work with the witchen' sticks, and they can make you feel ill if they are not meant for you. If you try to work with them and you feel hot and flushed, sick to your stomach, or get a bad headache or feel dizzy, then you need to put them down and leave them alone. They are not meant for you.

Sometimes I think spirit and the ancestors have jokes. Who would have thought I would have married a witchen' man? He is not into any type of spiritual workings at all. My mother-in-law was a worker and he stays clear of it—or so he says. Yet here he is, a witchen' man. He has worked on the pipeline since he first started to work. This is what he does for a living; he has a machine to find the underground lines, but it doesn't always work, for whatever reason. That is when he pulls out his witchen' sticks.

So I naturally asked him tons of questions, and I told him I was going to write about it in the book. Him not being "spiritual," I asked him if just anyone could pick up the rods or stick and find what they were looking for, and he said, "No!"

I said, "What do you mean, 'No'?"

He said that the sticks don't work for everyone because they don't understand them.

I said, "The people don't understand them?"

He said, "No, the witchen' sticks couldn't hear them."

I've been married to this man for almost forty years, and sometimes getting an answer out of him is tricky. Finally he says, "You gotta have a feel for them, and them for you"

"So the witchen' sticks have to have a connection with the person who is working them?"

"Yes."

"How do you do that?" I asked.

"You have to talk to them."

I was shocked!

"Do you speak out loud to them?" I asked.

He looked at me like I was crazy and said, "No! I tap them together and think of what I am looking for."

"Then what do you do?"

"I hold them loosely and I walk in the direction I think I should go. And if it is wrong, they will pull apart and let me know. Then I will think of moving the direction, and if it is the right direction they will show me by crossing or moving back and forth. You have to listen to them."

"Listen to who?"

"The sticks!"

Sweet baby Jesus on a stick. He's doing the same thing I do and doesn't even know it!

He went on to tell me that you have to be relaxed and clear your mind of all thoughts except for what you are looking for. He said he only looks for underground lines and that the flow of the line is what helps him find it. He said, "the witchen' sticks know what they are looking for."

"Do you use the same set every time?" I asked.

"No."

"Why not?" I said.

"When I use them a lot they get misplaced, so I just make more out of welding rods."

As all folks who work any type of divination knows, when a tool gets tired it just goes away. He's not a worker so he doesn't look at it that way. I knew he was getting tired of all my questions, but I had to push for just a little more because I wanted to understand how he works with them, yet he doesn't realize he is working with a divination tool.

I said, "So when you make another pair, do you just start using them?"

This man had the nerve to look at me like I fell off a truck and hit my head.

He said that he wipes the rods off; then he has to shape them. Once they are shaped, he cleanses them with water. Then he works them in his hands for a minute. Then they are ready to go.

I said, "Why do you do that?"

"That is what I was taught to do."

"Why do you work them before you use them?"

"So we can get to know each other."

So he's doing divination and doesn't even know it. He's cleansing his dowsing tool with cool water and he's holding it in his hands so their spirits can connect, although he would never say it like that. Then he goes and divines whatever he is looking for. My husband will never say it in a million years, but he is very gifted.

I've given you some information from regular folks; but what about divination Conjure style with witchen' sticks? I have always loved the idea of the witchen' sticks since I was a young child. I am still infatuated with them. You can't imagine the feel of spirit speaking through them unless you have worked with them. It is pure spirit! Spirit of place, the spirit of water, the spirit that is there but somehow we as humans miss it.

From what the ole folks say, this type of divination is not for everyone; not everyone has the gift that is needed to follow spirit this way. As we can see from my husband, you don't have to be a worker to be able to listen through spirit when working with the sticks. I say *sticks* because they can be wood or some type of rods. I don't think that the material really matters. My husband works with welding rods, I work with copper rods, my grandma had a tree branch shaped in a fork—I think what matters is the gift a person has to connect with spirit and to be able to listen and follow the subtle push that spirit gives when working with the witchen' sticks.

I treat my witchen' sticks just like I do any other divination tool. They have to be cleansed dressed, blessed, and given to the ancestors before they are worked with, because like any other tool of this sort, you are drawing your information from the ancestors and the spirits of place.

Before I move forward, I want to talk a little about what spirit of place means. Seasoned workers will already know, but what about others who may not be familiar with the term? As we know, the land holds a memory of the people who have lived and died upon it. The land carries the spirits of these folks. I believe that it is the spirits of place that helps us work with the witchen' sticks in divination. When you are working with this type of divination, you are depending solely upon the spirits that walk with you and the spirits of place.

Every home and every piece of land has its own spirits of place. It holds the memory of the past, and, as we know, without a past there could be no future. Like any other divination, you are dealing with spirit and should always be respectful. I have found when doing this type of divination to find out what types of spirits are in place. Not all spirits will come forward and want to be heard. So just to recap, spirit of place is all the spirits that live on a land. This could be human or animal spirits; it could be something that folks just passing through left behind. It is important that when you are doing this type of divination that you keep yourself spiritually protected, because you could be dealing with raw, untamed spirits. I'm not trying to scare you; I'm just simply stating the facts.

Any spiritual tool that I work with is given to my ancestors first. My witchen' sticks were no different. You can buy them already made or you can do like I did and make your own. Mine were made out of copper wire, I have always been drawn to copper. They can truly be made out of anything. I'll give instructions on how to make them later on, but first I want to talk about cleansing them and giving them to your ancestors so that spirit may speak through them. Once you get the material that you are going to be working with for your witchen' sticks, you need to run it through some cool running water. This will clear way any emotion from other folks that the material might have picked up. Once you have it cleansed, you are then ready to give it to your ancestors. Every divination tool that I own has been offered up and given to my ancestors; I'll share with you a small setup that you can do to fill your witchen' sticks with their spirit.

You will need:

- 3 red candles in glass
- A cool glass of water

- Some type of smoke
- A white handkerchief

Say your prayers as usual and call on your ancestors. Lay out the handkerchief and set your candles in the shape of a triangle, in this order: top, bottom left, bottom right. Place your witchen' sticks in the center of the triangle. Call on your ancestors again and petition them to come and sit with the witchen' sticks. Light the candles in the same order you set them down. Notice we went from left to right because we want to nail down the power of the ancestors in the sticks.

Light your smoke and offer it up, along with the glass of water, to the ancestors. Go back daily and say your prayers and your petitions over the sticks. Once the candles burn out, then, using a pendulum, test the power in the sticks. If the pendulum does not move well, then repeat the setup again. Once your sticks are ready, it is time to get to know them and to get used to the feel of them in your hands.

The more you work with the tool, the stronger your connection will become. You need to start out slow; don't try to rush this. It's like learning anything else—it takes time, patience, and practice. To start with, hold your witchen' sticks up to your mouth and say your name over them three times. Then blow three breaths over the sticks.

Hold the sticks in your hands and just relax. If you feel like you can't relax or that you are too anxious, then take three deep breaths and let them out slowly. Hold the sticks loosely and place your hands close together. (Some folks will keep a space between their hands; either way will work.)

You can test the sticks using your ancestor altar. Move away from your altar and petition the spirit in the witchen' sticks to help you find spirit in the room. Keep repeating this over and over in your mind until you reach your altar. Don't be surprised if they lead you somewhere else within the house. The most important thing is to not try to force it; be natural, be calm, and let your sticks show you what you are looking for. The sticks can be worked with for many different things: find things hidden in the yard, in the house—even things that are off within the body. You simply have to work with them and have a connection with them just like you would any other tool.

If you would like to make your own, you need some type of bendable wire. I prefer copper, but, like I said, my husband uses welding rods and he makes them as he goes. They seem to work well for him. You will need about a foot and a half of stiff wire, maybe a little longer, depending on how long you want your sticks. Some folks use the old wire clothes hangers—they simply snip the hanging part off and then bend the wire to fit in their hands. I tried that many years ago and didn't like the feel of it, but you may want to try that at first. When I was building mine, I offered the plain wire to my ancestors first and just did a small setup with three tea lights in a line behind the wire on my altar.

When the tea lights burned out I measured the palm of each hand to the wire and bent the wire where my hands felt comfortable. I then set my new sticks on the ancestor altar with another set of three tea lights. Once those tea lights burned out, I dressed my sticks with some holy oil and sent them out with three more tea lights. When the tea lights burned out, then I held a stick in my hands to see what my reaction would be to them and them to me. Once I saw that I wasn't going to be ill or feel funny, I offered them up to my ancestors. The witchen' sticks are just like any other tool that you work with, and you have to remember that sometimes we are not meant to be able to work with everything.

The witchen' sticks can be worked with for many different things nowadays; they are no longer just worked with to find water. Like everything else, things change with time, but the foundation stays the same. They can really be made any way you are comfortable with or with whatever material you choose. Just always remember that they are a tool with a spirit and they must be taken care of and respected—they are not a toy. Every so often, place them back on your ancestor altar to "feed" them so they will continue working well for you.

CONCLUSION

This is the end of the book, and it is my hope that the information shared will help the reader. Divination is a very large part of my professional practice. It is the very first place I start at before I begin any workings. It is important to know what is really going on when a client comes to me for help, and it is also important to know if I can really help them. If the reading says the job will be successful, that is great; but if it says there will be no success, then I either don't take the job or I try to find a different way to help them.

The first place to start is with your ancestors and some type of tool that you feel comfortable working with. Learn to listen to the spirits that walk with you because that is where the unseen is seen. I tried to share as much of my knowledge as I could so this work can live on. May your way always be opened.

ABOUT THE AUTHOR AND ILLUSTRATOR

STARR CASAS was born in the mountains of Kentucky and raised in the culture of the Deep South. A professional Conjure woman for over forty years, she is the co-owner of the shop Conjure New Orleans in the French Quarter and author of Old Style Conjure. A beloved teacher, she presents workshops across the United States. Visit her online at *www.oldstyleconjure.com*.

Born in New Orleans and raised in Marrero, Louisiana, JOSEF BAILEY has loved art for as long as he can remember. He began drawing at an early age and attended art school at the New Orleans Center for Creative Arts (NOCCA). Josef is a tattoo artist and works as an artist in the New Orleans area. He is also a float painter for Kern Studios Inc. and his artwork is on display during Mardi Gras.

TO OUR READERS

Weiser Books, an imprint of Red Wheel/Weiser, publishes books across the entire spectrum of occult, esoteric, speculative, and New Age subjects. Our mission is to publish quality books that will make a difference in people's lives without advocating any one particular path or field of study. We value the integrity, originality, and depth of knowledge of our authors.

Our readers are our most important resource, and we appreciate your input, suggestions, and ideas about what you would like to see published.

Visit our website at *www.redwheelweiser.com* to learn about our upcoming books and free downloads, and be sure to go to *www.redwheelweiser.com/newsletter* to sign up for newsletters and exclusive offers.

You can also contact us at *info@rwwbooks.com* or at
Red Wheel/Weiser, LLC
65 Parker Street, Suite 7
Newburyport, MA 01950